THE LIVELY SPIRITS OF PROVENCE

the lively spirits

Clarke, Irwin & Company Limited/Toronto, Vancouver

Jamie Brown

# of Provence

ISBN 0-7720-0718-7

1 2 3 4 5 6 JD 79 78 77 76 75 74

Printed in Canada

This book is for Jean-Pierre Brown.
He knows this story well.

THE LIVELY SPIRITS OF PROVENCE

1

It was the middle of September. The evening was dark and cool, and the waves on the English Channel had been rough. When we drove away from the grey docks, there had been confusing road signs and symbols that I had forgotten, and we had to drive on the right hand side of the road again, and the big French Citroën cars came wafting towards us with all their lights out. We wouldn't even know they were there until, when they were almost alongside us, the drivers would snap on the light switches, and the cars would blaze past in a scream of blinding yellow.

We fought the traffic through the centre of Boulogne. Everything was so different. Different from how I remembered it. All a bit frightening. And it wasn't until we were out of the city, past the string of small towns that straggle along the road near the city limits, and into the open country that we could relax. I was tired. There was a fog rolling in from the north, and I was determined to get to the hotel in St. Omer before it got worse, so I drove as fast as I dared on the bumpy, empty roads.

"Why are we driving so fast?" Lorna asked me, sitting straight up in her seat, clutching the handle on the dashboard.

"I want to get to the hotel ahead of the fog. We've come too far today. I'm tired," I said. "Why don't you relax and look out the window?"

She stared blankly out into the darkness. "It's really quite ugly, Jamie. It doesn't look nearly as charming as you said it would be."

"Don't worry," I said. "This whole part of the north is industrialized and ugly. But things will be better in the morning. When we get farther south. You'll see."

"Anyway, I can't see much if you're going to drive so fast."

"But everyone drives like this here," I said, excited by the sounds and smells of France we had just experienced, remembering roads just like this one I had driven on before. I had come back. And it was here that we had dreamed of finding a home. "It's really very French, you know, to drive fast and all. Don't worry. The French drivers are all very good."

We shot over the crest of a hill, and immediately tumbled out of the empty darkness into a blaze of high-powered lights, and confusion and cars stopped and people running on the road. I pulled up the car hard. And right away a man in a rough grey sweater darted through our headlights and around to our window. He shone a flashlight in on us and said very quickly in French, "Come and help!"

I was totally disoriented. A moment ago we had been speeding through blackened countryside totally alone, and now there were lights, and confusion, and a man with a flashlight talking to us through the window. Any French I ever knew crumbled and disappeared. "We . . . we are English," I finally said. The man rolled his eyes and threw up his hands and left. A great truck smoked up behind with its yellow lights blazing, nearly running into the back of us while trying to stop.

"We're safe now," I said. "We're protected from behind by that truck if anyone else comes over the hill. I'll go ahead and see what the trouble is. The road must be blocked. Maybe you'd better stay with the car."

About five cars up there was a wreck—sprawled sideways in a low spot on the road. Someone had rigged up some spotlights to help the rescuers see. It was too easy to see. Just past the wreck on the left hand side of the road was another car, upside down and in the ditch. There was broken glass everywhere. Smoke was curling up through the beams of the spotlights. An ambulance was coming up fast in the other direction. There were several people, either unconscious or dead, lying on the road, and there was one woman on the side of the road who was certainly dead. People stepped over her unnoticing and almost unaware of her lying there.

Volunteers and firemen were cutting swiftly through the roof of the Peugeot that was straddling the road. Cracking and peeling away at the roof, making giant sounds like someone peeling a walnut. And from inside the car, there was a woman calling for help. I hoped Lorna couldn't hear. There was nothing I could do. I was not French, and the police and the firemen and the ambulance had arrived. I went back to the car.

"Is it bad?" Lorna asked. "I can hear someone calling for help."

"It's bad. And I don't know what we can do to help. There's really nothing we can do. I think it would be best if we just got out of everyone's way. The road will be blocked for hours. We should turn around."

About a kilometer back down the road, we came to a crossroads we hadn't really noticed before because we had been going so quickly. A few whitewashed houses clustered together on the intersection, and people were gathering in front of the houses, their faces lit up by our headlights and the white glare of the accident.

We stopped to ask directions, and immediately the car was surrounded by curious villagers. "What has happened?" asked an old woman. "Is it an accident?" She clutched at her woollen shawl.

"Yes. A very bad accident. The road is blocked." I noticed that my French was coming back. "There is one dead. Maybe more."

The villagers' eyes widened in unison. "Ah! My God," somebody said.

"One dead!"

"Maybe more than one," the old lady said, crossing herself. "My God." A young mother in the crowd held up her sleepy child to see. The child didn't seem to understand what was going on. Everyone stared back down the road.

"We want to go to St. Omer," I said. "Is there another way to get there other than on this road?"

"But of course. Just go right . . ." said the old woman.

"Yes, right," a young man said.

"And then go left. Always to the left. It's not very far."

We left the villagers standing there, peering with white faces in morbid fascination, and headed back into the country. We climbed a steep hill on a winding, bumpy road, and the headlights reflected off the whitewashed trunks of the plane trees growing in corridors. I found myself driving very slowly indeed.

"I don't think I'm going to like France," Lorna said. "Not at all!"

2

The idea that I would someday live in France first came to me when I was five years old. It was the winter time, and I can remember sitting at the dining-room table as my father told us once again about his own stay there. At the table, he poured me a taste of dark red Burgundy, added a little water and stirred it with a great blunt finger. I tasted the wine as he told the stories.

Armed with his high-school French, he had gone straight from a small Ontario town to a sophisticated French university where he was a student for three years. The culture shock was tremendous. It influenced his thinking and his way of doing things all the rest of his life.

To him, Canada was a home, but France was a paradise. And we learned about wine and how to drink it at a time when wine was considered a sissy drink in Ontario, and anything other than "Old Grandma's Loganberry Winette" was virtually unattainable. We learned about eating, and we learned classic manners and Cartesian logic. But best of all, we sat at the table and felt the spirit that my father had captured, touching us.

In his three years he had uncovered the very essence of France. The key. And even now, with another generation governing the politics and the way of life, and with many ghosts still dying, that spirit is still true, and still the same.

I had been to France three times before. Lorna had never been. I came the first time in 1968 just at the beginning of the great national strike—the infamous "mai-juin." There was nothing anyone could do except sit in the cafés at night with lights flickering on and off as the electricity people reminded us all that they were on strike. I once bought some gas on the road at three in the morning for six dollars a gallon. We had been tipped off about the sale late in the afternoon. And even at that hour of the morning, there was a line-up. Everything was on strike.

Drugstores, hotels, airports, gas stations, customs, toll booths. I saw some rioters overturn a car in the street and set fire to it, and I took pictures of communist supporters attacking and occupying a factory in the north in the middle of the night. There was a lot of shouting, and bricks flying, and gunshots somewhere down the street. I remember being afraid.

I sent off some stories to a Canadian newspaper from England, since the French lines of communication were closed, then caught a boat back to France, and worked my way down to the south and lived for a while on a rice farm in the Camargue. It was a savage, flat, hot land, but the people there had a spirit and a classic grace that was as familiar to me as sitting at my father's table. The owner had two fierce geese living in his gateway acting most effectively as watchdogs.

I learned to love the country that time. And that love brought me back the following year on a sort of pilgrimage, almost as if to prove to myself once and for all that the good life and times and the friends that I had made really existed. Vivid impressions of the searing blue southern sky, the impossibly rugged landscape, the colour and character of the people had stayed with me hard and new. I was ready for a longer stay.

But when two people are first together, and both are young and trying to be artists, there is never enough money. Not even for simple necessities. Things like trips for two to France are so far out of the question, that it's surprising in retrospect that we even considered the idea.

Legally, Lorna and I were not married. It was impossible for us to be so, since Lorna had fled another marriage that had never really worked for her or her husband. It could have been a tragedy; but there were no children, no hard feelings, and no money involved. Lorna had come to me very poor, and we had held a secret ceremony together. And for a long time we simply lived with each other: married as far as we were concerned, and as far as anyone knew, and happy.

She was a striking woman even then, with straight, rich Indian hair and the softest possible brown eyes. Her skin was dark and clear, even in winter. And the way she carried herself and the way she moved her slick dancer's body as she talked, you could tell she was an actress. Through and through.

Lorna and I were living in a large and rather uninteresting second-floor flat in one of the toughest districts in Toronto. We never did without, at least not that I can remember, but we often pooled resources with friends to make a good big meal. One friend would have some flour and some onions, another would have some potatoes and meat, and another would have some beer or a bottle of wine. We would get together like that to have a feast. At least once a week. And there were plenty of times that we didn't have any money at all. Especially around rent day. Then we would go around the flat pilfering butts out of the ashtrays to roll new cigarettes, and savouring the warm yeasty smell in the air from the bread factory down the street. But those times weren't as bad as they might sound.

While we lived in Toronto, Lorna worked long hours in the theatre, where everyone was either making pots of money or none at all. Mostly none at all. And I was wrestling with my novel.

Things were not going well. I had been writing in Canada for some time, and thought I was used to it, but it was the sum total of the experience that finally finished me off. Over the period of several years, I began to feel the subtle pressures of a whole series of literary people and businesses who weren't interested and who wouldn't answer letters; of Arts Councils who didn't seem to want to cooperate, telling me instead "not to feel personally slighted" as they turned me down once again; of cocktail friends and lawn party acquaintances whose sole interest in me and my projects was how much money I wasn't making, and when I was going to give up and come to my senses. Like everyone else.

I felt that pressure in Toronto. Toronto was costing me money, and I wasn't making anything in return. Insurance salesmen and house painters scoffed at the basic folly of our economic situation. God help the other artists our age. Most of them were worse off than we were. Bank tellers in rhinestone-studded glasses sneered at our paltry bank account, and consulted in loud voices with the bank manager about the wisdom of allowing a joint account in their bank for two consenting adults of different sexes with different names.

Eventually, my work stopped altogether. Leaving me high and dry and in the middle of a novel which I would never finish. Leaving me frightened and shaken.

This had not been in the scheme of things. There had never been any plan for such an emergency. And instead of worrying about what I should do, I worried about what people would think. About what I would tell them. How I would explain.

I had plenty of time to myself. Plenty of time to struggle through the snow during the worst winter in living memory, and time to do all the shopping for both of us. I bought most of our groceries at a supermarket nearby. Not any worse than any of the others I tried. I bought spinach in plastic bags from a gum-chewing checkout girl, and green tomatoes, and dazzling white chicken sandwiched between layers of cellophane and cardboard so that I couldn't smell, taste or touch it.

We couldn't find bread anywhere in the city that was consistently good or fresh, so we finally decided to bake our own. I had time all right. Time to notice and reflect on all these problems.

And food wasn't the only difficulty: we borrowed a television set that didn't work too well, and had a gas stove that wasn't reliable, and an American car that simply didn't run. When we visited my parents at Christmas time, their dish washer had flooded the kitchen, the furnace was out of order, both of their radios were dead, and the telephone was working only sporadically. North America may lack a lasting culture of its own, we figured, the United States may be smouldering in a dying dream, Canada may be crying for roots and a place in history, but we have always felt superior to the world in one way at least: we've been hopelessly smug about our vast wilderness of technological miracles.

It wasn't as if Lorna and I scoffed at all the materialism around us, and strutted off like ageing drop-outs to live a simple country existence away from all the gimmicks and gadgetry. We weren't as idealistic as that. But we did find it hard to be smug about a bunch of miracles that didn't work. And for that reason, we didn't find it hard to search for something new and more valuable in our lives than simple acquisitions.

Lorna liked Toronto for her work. Although it wasn't paying well, there was plenty of it. I found it hard. But Toronto was foreign to both of us as a place to live, and both of us were bothered by the usual big-city problems of excessive noise and air pollution. Other things disturbed us as well. We hated to see the simple courtesies of life forgotten. We were tired of being bullied by bus drivers. We were tired of eating spongy green peppers and seasonless salads. Any fruit or vegetable could be bought at any time—if you were prepared to pay the price. We were even tired of the weather.

And all the time we were there—together in our bed with the weekend papers on a Saturday afternoon, or at any time—I would talk about the France I knew. My personal promised land. I talked about it and reminisced about it, and compared the life there with the life we were living, until Lorna buckled under the barrage of information and unexpectedly began nodding her head in all the right places. Suddenly she was wanting to go there as much as I was. And the idea became ours instead of mine.

We were living theatre hours then. Breakfast at one o'clock, lunch at four or five, and dinner at eleven or twelve midnight. And lots of nights, after dinner, we lay in bed in the room with the blue walls, and heard the sounds of winter outside, and we read about France. We pored over everything we could find about the "lost generation" who lived in Paris during the twenties. We felt the romance of the era and the city it happened in. We studied maps and read about the soil, and the hospitals, and the economy, and the artistic climate, and the standard of living. So that over a period of several months we came to be minor authorities on the country, at least in our own circle of friends.

"But there's one real hassle," she said. "I wouldn't be able to work there."

"Why not?"

"Well how can I possibly act when I can't even speak the language?"

"How about mime?" I said, jokingly.

"Don't be ridiculous."

"Well . . . I could work . . . and you could take some time off!"

"Oh great. So my career doesn't count then?"

"No, no. It's not that. You're working now, and I'm not getting anything done. So we could move over there, and I could work and you wouldn't do anything for a change."

"Is that the way you've been figuring it?"

"It's my turn," I said.

"Well, if we ever get to France, we're not going to forget about my career. That's got to be part of the deal. I'd miss acting. It's a part of me and a part of my life, just like writing's a part of yours. We'll have to agree to come back eventually so that I can take up where I left off."

"That's fair enough."

We began to save everything we could. Lorna got into a big musical and everything she made from that we put into the bank. At the same time that she was doing the musical, she was earning a small regular salary doing a children's show that toured Toronto schools, and we spent that money on groceries.

Later on, when it was warmer, I started a large vegetable garden on my father's farm, and we began visiting their home more and more often as the weekends got warmer. We grew enough vegetables to keep ourselves in groceries for the entire summer, and my parents and our friends as well. The land was good at the farm. It nearly killed me turning it by hand, because the soil in the spot we chose hadn't been turned for fifty years. But I turned it anyway, and we found magic pieces of pottery two feet down in the ground.

And one night when the spring was upon us wet and heavy, Lorna came home from a show and collapsed. Toronto was killing us both. Under doctor's orders, Lorna was forced to give up working for a year. So we moved out to the farm, and looked after the house there while my parents were away, and ate fresh chemical-free vegetables, and felt the sun, and I watched Lorna grow healthy and brown and look better than she had all winter.

And by the time summer was under way, a cheque had arrived in the mail for me, for something I had written some time before. One thousand beautiful dollars. It was the last money I could count on earning from writing for the next ten months, but it broke the back of our savings plan. It put us over the hump. We knew that sometime later in the summer, and for some length of time that we couldn't really be sure of, we would be in France.

But there was one other complication. During a routine checkup at the doctor's, Lorna learned the real reason that she was growing so healthy and brown: she was pregnant!

"How do you feel?" I asked.

"Never felt better."

"Sure?"

"Sure," she said, smiling. "Except that I am a little worried about one thing."

"The travelling?" My heart sank.

"No. Not that. It's just that . . . we're not legally married. Something could happen. Who knows? We might want to have the baby over there."

In a way, we were hamstrung by the laws of the land, and I felt mildly frustrated. "Listen. We've only one immediate problem. And that's money. If we can't raise some more money somewhere, our relocation to France will end up being a day-trip to Montreal." She still looked worried. "Besides, nine months is a long time. We can't just sit on our hands waiting it out worrying. Things will be different by then. Let's go! Live! While the going's good."

Coincidentally, within the week we heard from her husband's lawyers. They told us that he was going ahead and filing for divorce. There was no worry about it costing us money, they said. Just sign the papers they were sending us, and the court proceedings would go on in our absence. There was hardly a chance that anything could go wrong. Everything would be over with by October 12th. After that, providing there hadn't been any hitches, we would be free to marry or do whatever we wanted. We signed. Everyone was happy.

To us, a legal marriage had meant little. We had said our secret ceremony. But now, with a baby coming and a divorce imminent, the conditions had changed entirely.

"But that's the beauty of the deal," I told her. "After the twelfth, we'll be able to get married quickly, easily and without any fuss. Anytime we feel like it."

"Who wants to get married?" she said, playfully.

"I do! I want the baby to be legally ours."

"He'll be ours in any case."

"No," I said. "I've found out that I won't be his legal guardian unless we're married. I want him to be ours in every way: not just ours as far as you and I are concerned." I was feeling terribly fatherly and responsible.

"If we get married after the twelfth, I want to string out our stay in France and have the baby there." She sounded as if she'd made her mind up long ago.

"We might not have enough money to last that long."

"We'll make it last," she said. "We might as well do this thing right. French obstetrical care is world famous. And besides, if our baby were born there, he'd be a dual citizen, wouldn't he?"

"I think so."

"Your father's always been a spiritual citizen of France, Jamie. He'd be very proud. And it could be a great advantage. A gift we could give our baby."

"He could be bilingual as well! That's an advantage too."

"Don't you think it'd be worth it?"

"It'd be worth it," I said. "You're right. We'll hang on no matter what."

"No matter how little money we have?"

"No matter."

Things began to happen fast. We discovered a cheap one-way charter flight to London for the 2nd of September. London wasn't the south of France, but it was on the right side of the ocean, and the charter was Bargain City. So we sent off a cheque in the mail as quickly as we could, and when the tickets finally arrived, and we could touch them, we felt truly committed. There was no turning back. Our precious money was spent. There would be no worrying about courtroom decisions. From then on anything we did, everything we spent or saved, had something to do with the trip.

Just two weeks before we were supposed to go, I calculated that we still didn't have enough money. Especially now that my travelling companion was pregnant and determined to stay abroad to have her baby. So I pulled on my oldest clothes and went to work in a friend's machine shop. Whenever my finances ran precariously low, I managed somehow to convince my friend that I was needed. And I'd squeeze in the door once more and assume my labours as junior apprentice and lathe hand.

On September 1st, we consolidated all the money. I borrowed $500 from a friendly banker, emptied our bank accounts, collected old debts, paid off new ones, sold anything we hadn't already sold, and with $1,952.63 in hand, we stepped onto the plane.

3

The bells were just ringing 11:00 p.m. as we rattled through the lighted main square of St. Omer, and turned down to the Hôtel du Commerce. On the sidestreet, the streetlamps cast pale Degas cones of light down into the shifting fog. We were both hungry and exhausted. Whatever excitement we might have felt had melted away with the accident; and the constant ugliness of the area was occasionally discernible through the fog, plunging Lorna's spirits lower still. The tiny $400 car we had bought in England was almost out of gas. We nudged it up over a curb across the street from the hotel, parked, and climbed the hotel steps beside a single lighted window.

Sitting behind a large wooden desk, surrounded by pens and official looking documents, was a grey-faced, severe-looking woman. She peered at us over the tops of her glasses and studied us disapprovingly as a great aunt might have studied us if we hadn't washed properly for the dinner table. A row of polished brass keys jangled behind her on a wooden board.

"Bonjour," I said, blowing the whole thing right off the bat.

"Bonsoir," she corrected. I felt like slinking back for another try at my hands.

"We would like a room for the night," I said. "Something comfortable and interesting. But not too expensive. We are artists. We are not exactly rich."

It's terribly North American to get right down to the nitty-gritty. Immediately dispel any mystery by running through a capsulated version of your life history and the state of your financial affairs. Madame behind the desk smiled unexpectedly, and softened. I smiled a bit myself, knowing full well that although I was being hopelessly North American, I was certain to arouse feelings of kinship and approval in an old-guard French person by being frankly cheap.

"We have just the room for you, Monsieur. You may inspect it if you wish. It's 14 francs a night." She reached around to the wooden board and handed me a large brass key. "Upstairs," she said. "To the right."

As we struggled up the stairs in the pitch dark, I did a quick mental calculation. "Fourteen francs, Lorna—that's only $2.70!"

"The room must be awful," she replied.

We groped down the hallway and felt our way to the room. I explained to Lorna that no French hotel with any character at all would waste money by turning on the overhead lights. We opened the door with some difficulty, and snapped on the lamp.

The room was fantastic. There was an enormous antique bed that had been built for some giant of another age. An ornate table in the centre of the room flirted four gracefully curved legs that wouldn't have been out of place in a pre-Revolution château. In one corner was an armoire with little shelves and drawers and mirrors, and a place to hang clothes about the size of a closet. In the other corner was a sink.

We closed the door again, and headed down the hall, chuckling and nudging each other over the great bargain we had discovered. And halfway down the hall, we stopped and looked out the window, down into the inner courtyard of the hotel. Its flower pots and skylights and cobblestones were all pale blue in the moonlight.

"Very well, Madame. I'll take the room. It's satisfactory."

"Ah good." She seemed immensely pleased. She patted a hair back into the bun on the top of her head, and straightened her ancient grey sweater. Then she asked me for my passport, and copied down all the particulars that everyone always seems to have to know in Europe.

"I want to park my car in your courtyard," I said. I liked to do that in the north. Someone told me once that there was a rash of petty thievery there, although I'd never come across any myself.

"Oh, but Monsieur. It's quite expensive. It would cost you one franc a night to have it locked up!"

"Hang the expense!" I said. "I want my car safe."

"But . . . but of course, Monsieur. As you wish." She looked at me disparagingly, over the tops of her glasses again, as if I were being rather reckless and silly. I realized that I had gone back down considerably in her estimation.

"One more thing, Madame. I know it's quite late, but we haven't eaten yet this evening. Can we get something to eat in the hotel?"

"Yes. We'll keep the dining room open for you. But you must hurry and park your car and do whatever is necessary before eating." She glanced at the man's wristwatch she was wearing. "It's late. Try to be in the dining room within an hour."

French menus have always looked bewildering to me, even after months of looking at them. There are inevitably some things on the menu that I can't identify. And by the time I have looked over the apéritifs, entrées and à la cartes, I can't tell the difference between a tourist plate and the plate of the day. Naturally it was even more difficult when I had to figure out everything for someone else as well. Poor Lorna couldn't understand a word of French.

At exactly a quarter to twelve, the white-jacketed waiter pushed through the swinging kitchen door. He picked his way through the empty dining-room, whisking crumbs nonchalantly off a vacant table here and there, and finally arrived at our table with his pen poised and one eyebrow raised.

I started confidently at the top of the menu, having prepared for him in advance, and pointed out the various things we would like, savouring each dish as I mentioned it. Curiously, the more I ordered as I went down the list the less the waiter seemed to be writing, until eventually he wasn't writing at all. Something had gone wrong.

When I had finally finished, he smiled and bent down and said in his most confidential voice, "If you please, Monsieur, let me help you order. I am afraid you have made a mistake."

"But of course. What's wrong?"

"If Monsieur looks over on the other side of the card, he will see that everything that he has ordered is listed on the tourist menu. If you order from the tourist side of the menu, you can have exactly the same thing for two-thirds the cost."

My self-image as a great gourmet, sending back the potatoes and sniffing discriminately at the wine, collapsed like a careless soufflé. But Monsieur in the white coat was a professional waiter, and typically French. He was neither ingratiating, nor condescending, nor apologetic. He simply couldn't give a damn. He just smiled and shrugged and evidently considered his suggestion all in a night's work.

Twenty minutes later, after an apéritif and black olives and the first French bread I had eaten in three years, the waiter carried in a steaming entrée. Four of the largest artichokes that we had ever seen. Then he brought to the table a small silver boat into which he poured oil and vinegar and shavings of garlic and onions and other things that we couldn't identify, and he mixed them all lovingly, carefully, skilfully. And when he was done, he delicately spooned the nectar into shallow dishes for us, and stood there, beaming, waiting to be congratulated while we touched the first green leaf of artichoke to the sauce.

Later on, he brought out two trout that had been grilled in smoking almonds, and with perfect skill he sliced each fish along its belly, and lifted out all the bones in one sure swift motion. We were left breathless.

I watched Lorna with delight all through the meal. She liked eating as much as I did, and the meal was raising her spirits. It was everything I had described to her. She sampled her first French bread, and wrinkled her nose as she tried it, unable to give an opinion one way or the other on it. I knew she would learn to love it in time. I watched her out of the corner of my eye as the waiter prepared the sauce for the artichoke. She was trying not to look astonished. I watched her try the trout and exclaim about it in shining whispers. It made me very happy.

We lay in our giant's bed later on, full of good food. We left the casement windows open, and listened to the night sounds outside the window. And just before we fell asleep, we heard the bells in the tower down the street beating out a complicated, out-of-step, quaint little song, with one bell that was hopelessly out of tune. We wondered if they could hear us giggling together down the hall.

4

Even today, a lot of rural France is abandoned countryside. In the south, picturesque peasant's cottages nestle unused and empty in the vineyards, and enterprising farmers have bought up great châteaux to use as barns. The grand ballrooms where counts and even kings once danced are now often filled to the chandeliers with grain. And in the mountains, whole villages perch abandoned with doors and shutters flopping, overlooking staggering views of the Mediterranean a hundred miles or so away. Complete villages are up for sale.

It was not always this way. But the French have suffered a great deal from the effects of two world wars; perhaps more than most people realize. Vast numbers of young men were cut down in the First World War, and then before France had a chance to recover, more were killed in the Second. A great number of potential fathers were eliminated.

The result is that there are hardly more people living in France today than there were at the turn of the century. And on top of that, the rural areas have suffered a tremendous migration of people to the cities. This has left a good deal of the countryside empty.

While we were in Toronto, we read about this problem. We read about all sorts of houses left abandoned in every corner of the country, but especially in the south. We learned that the owners of these houses have been placed in a dilemma. Either pay the taxes to the government on their unused property, and classify it as a habitable dwelling, or tear the roof off of it, and class the stark remains as unusable acreage. When you are aware of the national passion in France for, shall we say, watching pennies, it is not so surprising to discover roofless houses at every turn in the road.

But nowadays, the owners have a third opportunity. They can

get a very low interest loan from the government through an organization called the Fédération Nationale des Gîtes de France for restoring the old houses. Sometimes they can even wangle a pure grant. Especially if the building is historically interesting.

When the restoration is complete, the Gîtes people come down and give the accommodation an inspection. And their inspection is truly rigorous. Each house or apartment must have electricity in every room, electric lights, a stove, a water closet meeting the strict rural codes, fuel for the fireplace or furnace, dishes, cutlery, blankets for the bed. Everything in fact to make a tenant's stay comfortable.

The idea is simple. The government is delighted to receive all the increased tax revenues from habitable houses, and perhaps even more delighted at the thought of potential tourist dollars flowing into the country. Especially into the impoverished rural areas.

And the result is unique. There are 12,000 accommodations available, usually at the lowest prices you can find anywhere in the country. And the entire 12,000 are listed in a book published annually by the non-profit, government-subsidized Gîtes organization in Paris.

Naturally, we sent for the book, wiring four dollars by International Money Order to Paris. And we spent many winter nights poring over the pages, discovering bargains, dreaming about the different areas of France. We found that the 12,000 possibilities were scattered throughout seventy-six of France's ninety-five départements. We were astonished to find every home described in detail, with the furnishings, the rooms, the size, the method of heating, all mentioned explicitly. Even the exteriors of the gîtes and the quality of the view from the windows were remarked upon.

We found a cottage with lounge, terrace, bedroom, kitchen and small garden situated very near the Mediterranean that could be rented for $17.50 a week. And a rambling Normandy farmhouse on substantial land, with a lounge, dining-room, large open fireplace and bedrooms to sleep eight in comfort could be rented for $40 a week. The possibilities were endless.

There was, of course, a great price spread, depending on the type of accommodation and the area that it was in. Fashionable spots were commanding sky-high rents. And naturally, during the high season, the prices were steep all over the country. But I knew even then that France was no longer a cheap place to live. You can't go there with the idea of saving money any more. You have to go for other reasons. It costs as much as Canada now, and in many ways even more. So the rents in the off-season seemed remarkably low to me.

After days of rattling indiscriminately through the book, we became more selective. The novelty of a bargain pure and simple was wearing off. I knew most of the départements, or at least the area in which the départements could be found, so I had a general idea of the topography and climate of each place we considered.

"How about the Hautes Alpes?" Lorna would ask in our bedroom with the ice-blue walls.

"Too cold. Also it might be hard to drive around in the winter. The roads are really mountainous and winding."

"What about Gard?"

"It's nice. A little savage and flat maybe. But that's where I lived before. Remember? I want to see something new. We can leave it in reserve if you like, just in case we don't find anything else."

We finally settled on two areas that had everything we wanted: the Vaucluse and the Dordogne. I had been through the Vaucluse plenty of times, and had always thought it would be one of the finest places on earth to live. The Dordogne was a second choice. I had never been there, but every expert on France that I knew talked in loving, ecstatic terms about it. An American writer I know was so enchanted that he bought some land there so that when he retires some twenty years from now, he can move to the Dordogne and build a house. But for us, the Vaucluse was number one.

The next thing we had to consider was our finances. It didn't take us long to decide that we couldn't afford anything over $120 a month. And in a high-priced area like the Provence, that eliminated the majority of the possibilities right away. We crossed them out of the book.

Lorna and I had never lived in a house. Not our own. It had always been a crowded apartment or part of a larger house. All we really wanted was a place of our own. Preferably in the country. So we took out a pen and recklessly scratched out every single apartment in the Vaucluse.

Now our list was narrowed down to only a few dozen places.

And it was while studying these and trying to determine which ones were adequately heated for winter living, that Lorna discovered the most significant category of all. A tiny asterisk was listed in the legend in French, but in the short explanatory page in English at the front of the book, it was not mentioned at all. It was a symbol for a "gîte de caractère." We laughed in delight at the discovery, and pretended that it was a deliberate plot on the part of the editors not to mention the gîtes de caractère in the English legend. We decided that it had been a subtle conspiracy to save those special gîtes for the French and the knowledgeable few.

"Why don't we write and reserve a house before we leave?" she asked. "There mightn't be anything available when we get there."

"I doubt if that would happen. The tourist season is all wrapped up by the middle of September. There should be lots of places. Besides, I'm damned if I'm going to rent some place I haven't even seen. We don't even know how accurate this book is."

"But what if there really aren't any places?"

"We've got our tent, haven't we? We'll find a place even if it takes some time. We'll have to take chances, that's all."

"Some chances! I'm the one who's pregnant."

"But you have to take risks to get anything worthwhile," I said. ". . . Of course, if you're afraid, we could always stay here."

She turned and looked straight at me, framed in the window with the light shining in behind her, glowing yellow on the tips of her dark hair. "I'm ready to go when you are," she said.

When we left the hotel in St. Omer, we headed unhurriedly through the morning fog, more or less in the direction of the Vaucluse. We planned to take a week just getting there from the north, and then spend as much time as we needed to find a house that cost $120 a month or less, had good heating, and had . . . character. And there were only two! One in Lourmarin, and one in Gigondas. Both were villages we had never seen.

5

The sun was staring its traditional Provençal blue as we wrestled up the narrow road to the tiny village of Lourmarin. It hadn't been an easy place to find. It was so small that most of the maps had forgotten it, and we had to ask directions several times.

It was early morning. We were creaking rheumatically from spending a week in our tent and several nights in lumpy hotels, and we were looking forward to finding our little house.

The road was potted and patchwork and full of turns, but even at a distance we could see Lourmarin shining through the trees. Just to see it like that made the drive worthwhile. It was a true mountain town, dominated by an enormous château at one end, and in the morning light the walls of Lourmarin looked orange-yellow.

We came in from the south end of the village, and almost immediately the walls closed in on us, making it difficult to drive the car. The street narrowed down and squeezed us in, until we were practically scraping the door handles on the walls of the houses, as the road serpentined through the orange buildings at crazy angles. It was almost claustrophobic.

Suddenly, the street widened again into a small sunny Place with a fountain splashing happily into an ancient green basin. There was one other car in the place, and we pulled up beside it, taking the only other parking space that we could see in the entire centre of the village.

I looked at the Gîte book. "It says the address is the Place de l'Eglise," I said. "This is probably it. Especially because there's a church at one end."

"We can't go any farther anyway," said Lorna.

Up the street in the sunlight three elderly ladies appeared smiling in spotted dresses, struggling under a load of boxes, suitcases, bags. They seemed to be truly in love with their village, for as they came towards us they would pause periodically to examine things in the street, or breathe the clear air appreciatively, or feel the warmth already rising from the yellow stones.

"Those women will be able to give us directions," I said. When they were very near, I called out the window. "S'il vous plaît, Mesdames. . . ."

"Good heavens," said the first woman in perfect English. "What on earth are you doing here?"

Manicured English syllables were the last thing we expected to hear in a tiny square in a small, isolated Provençal village. We hadn't heard English for more than a week.

"Are you from London?" asked the first lady, smiling.

"No . . . we're Canadians," Lorna answered. I was still too surprised to speak.

"Oh. How wonderful! But we thought you were English because you have English registration plates on your car."

"No," I said. "We really are Canadians. We bought the car in England."

"Jolly good!" said the third lady, and she clapped her hands together delightedly. "We're from the south of England ourselves. You two are the first English-speaking people we've heard in over a month."

"But what on earth are you doing here?" the first lady asked again.

"We're looking for a house to rent," Lorna said. "We've read about Lourmarin in our guide books."

"Oh, it's a wonderful place," she said. "We've been staying here for a month every year for the past five years. We rent a house here, you see. You'll love it!"

"Is this the Place de l'Eglise?" I asked.

"Yes it is," they all said, nodding their straw hats.

"Then we've come to the right place." I picked up the guide book. "We're looking for a Madame Chauvin. Do you know her?"

"Why yes! Of course we do. She's our landlady, and our great friend."

"Then you must be renting the house we've been looking for!" said Lorna.

"We must be. I'm sure it's the only house she owns other than her own. What a remarkable coincidence!"

"You may be in luck too," said the first lady. "We're leaving for England today. That's why we have these suitcases. You may be able to rent the house starting tomorrow."

Madame Chauvin was an elegant French lady in a patterned green dress and red hair, like a character actor from a bad Greek movie. She brought us in to her cool, dark front hall by the very ancient doorway, and after a little conversation, she told us with great regret that her house was not vacant at all, as the English ladies had thought it might be. It was rented for another month. But after that, it would be free.

"We are sorry to have called on you so early in the morning, Madame. But we're very anxious to find a house. It's been our dream for some time."

"It is nothing, Monsieur," she said. "You are both very charming. If you can't find anything else, do come back."

"We will, Madame." We left the cool, dark hallway then for the sunny place; the ghastly idea of living in the tent for a month waiting for the new tenants to move out ran through my mind.

We were disappointed. But we were absolutely crushed when we saw the house that might have been. The three ladies invited us down to inspect it so that we might have an idea of what to expect in other houses that we tried to rent.

It was off the street and below it, and we entered the house from one side through a leafy archway. The rooms were monastic inside, with arched, vaulted ceilings and black oak beams, gnarled and distorted from centuries of dry rot. The walls were painted white.

"It used to be a laundry at one time," said one of the ladies.

"It's sixteenth century," said another.

"The laundry for the large house that Madame Chauvin lives in."

"The house has been in the family for a long time."

There was another doorway off the kitchen, and it led out to a tiny courtyard that was dappled with sunlight and crowded with the plants of Provence. In the middle of the yard was a stone table, shaded by an arching fig tree whose branches were so heavy with ripe figs that they bent down till they almost touched the table top.

"We often eat out here," one lady remarked proudly. "We think it's very pleasant, especially when it's hot."

Three English ladies, with matching hats, straight out of

Somerset Maugham. They had brought their tea and biscuits and jam with them from England. Enough to last for a month. And they served us tea in the old laundry, even though it was just mid-morning. They told us that the village of Lourmarin had been the home of Albert Camus for some time.

"His house is just down the road from ours," one lady said.

"They say his widow still comes here occasionally."

We sipped our Twining's Earl Grey, and nodded. We were both very sad that we couldn't rent the house. I could see Lorna's grainy disappointment in the antique mirror across the room.

"What are you going to do now?" the second lady asked.

"We'll go up to the village of Gigondas," I answered. "Have you ever heard of it?"

"No."

"There's another house there we want to see. We may be able to rent that one."

"But I'm sure it won't be as exciting as yours," Lorna said.

"So am I," I said.

The Mistral is one of the most famous winds in the world. It has been raking through Provence, and influencing the lives of men there since the beginning of recorded history. It springs out of nowhere, and screeches down the Rhône-Saône corridor like an express train. A friend in the south once told me that "Mistral" means "master." It is the Master Wind. And when it blows, he told me, it keeps on blowing for three, six or nine days. It is the subject of many poems, the moaning background for many novels, and the name of a very fast Italian sports car. They say the wind has driven people mad.

And when we left Lourmarin for Gigondas, the Mistral wound around us without warning and bucked and bobbed our little car, tossing it playfully all over the road. The Mistral grasses and cypress hedges, that were planted around the fields for protection, were bending furiously in the wind, fighting to stay erect. They looked like rows of dust mops, being shaken and clattered out of shuttered windows. In the low areas, where the road runs alongside the canal between Lourmarin and l'Isle-sur-la-Sorgue, the fields were all protected. And the fences and cypress and Mistral grasses were planted in rows, running in right angles and other angles around the fields. We decided that the area must be a notorious one for wind.

But when we turned north, the weather suddenly improved, and the air was still. We moved through the corridors of plane trees, and splashed in and out of sunlight. We saw olives, figs, kaki, apples and lemons growing. And everywhere we looked, we could see grapes.

We passed through the partially fortified city of Carpentras, and darted under the aqueduct. Then the countryside became wilder, and the road narrower and full of turns. A high grey range of mountains stretched across the horizon on our right. And closer up were lower mountains with grey rocks and shrubs of mossy blue-green. Ancient grey ruins crumbled through the trees on the tops of many of the lower mountains. On our left, the yellow land sloped gently towards the Rhône, and it was very flat. The mountains ended so abruptly that it seemed as if the road were a boundary line between the mountains and the plains.

Finally we saw the turn for Gigondas, and we followed a twisting little lane to the right of the main road, and up into the first series of mountains.

When we came to a rise in the road, just beside a great wine house, we had our first view of Gigondas. We could see the tiny mediaeval town, high above the vineyards, scratched dramatically across the side of a mountain. The old town was lying in ruins above the new town. Enormous, arching fortifications teetered high up, left from the Middle Ages. We could understand immediately how as the times became safer and more civilized, the village had gradually migrated down the hillside to a more convenient and less precarious position.

We stopped there by the vineyards and studied the town looming above us through the leaves and the silence. And we both felt a strange excitement about the place. At that moment, we were sure that we had finally found a home.

6

As far as we could see, there was just one street in the village of Gigondas that was navigable by automobile, and it ended abruptly in a square by a Roman fountain. It was noon. There was no one to be seen in the entire village. The shutters on every house were fastened tight against the blazing heat, and we knew that at that very moment behind the shutters all over the south of France, everyone was sitting down to a three-hour lunch.

We swung the car around in the place, edging carefully past the fountain and rumbled back down the main street. A very old, spotted dog was sprawled under the sign for the bakery.

"We could ask directions there," Lorna said. "Bakers always know where everyone lives."

"Good idea."

We pulled up just across from the dog, and against the wall. Right from the car we could see down and out onto the plains below the village for about twenty-five or thirty miles. We could see a river that we didn't know, and patchworks of vineyards, and one or two blue ranges of mountains in the distance to the west, well on the other side of the Rhône.

Gigondas. A strange name for a village even in French. A corruption of the Roman "jocunditas." A name we had struggled with for months before we had ever seen the village.

"I like it here," Lorna said suddenly. "It's even better than I thought it would be. I hope we can live here."

"Look up the name and address of the man we want to find, then."

"I already have," she answered, excited. "It's Henri Barruol, and the address is the Domaine de St. Cosme."

"If it's a domaine, it must be a fairly large property. Even an estate. What's the street address?"

"There isn't any."

"Then I'll have to ask."

Nobody was even thinking about lunch inside the bakery. It was cramped and clanking with noise and heat. The two men working in the half-light of the baking room were stripped to the waist. They wore caps to keep the sweat out of their eyes. At the far end of the room was a gaping open-hearth oven carved into the wall, with orange flames reaching and roaring out the door.

I asked the older man with the grey hair if he knew the Domaine de St. Cosme. "But of course, Monsieur!" he shouted over the noise. He wiped his brow, and took off his hat, and brushed his floured hands on his pants. "Come outside," he said. I followed him into the sunlight and the quiet. He took me down the street a few paces where we could see better. His face still floured white.

"Do you see that fork in the road there?" His southern accent strong and musical.

"Yes," I said.

"Just take that fork, and pull into the yard by the great house at the bottom of the hill. It's the very first turn after the fork."

I thanked the baker for coming away from his work to show us the way. "I am at your service, Monsieur," he replied. "Besides, it's pleasant to get out of the shop for a moment."

We followed the bend to the right as instructed, and turned immediately into a tree-lined laneway. We passed a painted sign that said "Domaine de St. Cosme," standing in a clump of rosemary. Lorna stayed in the car near the fountain, cool under the shade of the plane trees. She crossed her fingers, she told me later, hoping we had finally found our house.

From the top of the steps I could hear nothing. My knocks echoed down a long hallway inside, but there were no sounds of anyone coming. I could feel the sun hanging on my back. Very suddenly, the great door opened and from the near darkness inside stepped a short, grey-haired, ordinary-looking man in ordinary-looking clothes. He regarded me calmly through his slightly tinted glasses and said nothing. He was still chewing something from his dinner table. And right then, I knew I was already on the wrong footing with him. We had been over-anxious, and tired, and wanted to find a house too badly. And I knew we had committed an unpardonable sin. We had disturbed him during his lunch.

"If . . . if you please, Monsieur, I am looking for a Monsieur Barruol."

"That's me," he said, still chewing, his arms resting at his sides.

"I . . . understand you have a house that you rent. Is it available now?"

"It might be," he answered, aloof.

Now I was *sure* I was on the wrong footing. "Well, I know you are very occupied with your lunch just now," I said. "And I apologize for having arrived at your door at such an inconvenient hour. But if the house might still be rented after your lunch is finished, perhaps we could return."

Monsieur Barruol grinned up at me unexpectedly. "Come on," he said. "I'll show you the house."

"But your lunch . . . ."

"It can wait. There is always time. Follow me. I'll show you the way." Without saying a word to the people he had left at the table, he sprinted down the front steps, and jumped into his upright Peugeot sedan, and sped off along the forked road. Away from Gigondas.

Monsieur flashed up and around the first few bends, pushing his car to the limit. We followed as well as we could, serpentineing up and under the shadow of an eleventh-century Romanesque chapel that stood high in his fields on the left. We were at once away from any houses, driving flat out along the bottim of a narrow valley lined with vineyards. High up above us on the right were the great grey rock formations that tourists come hundreds of miles to see. We found out later that they are called the Dentelles, which means lace in English. But they jab three hundred feet straight up into the air along the crest of a mountain, and to us, they looked more like the ragged teeth of a saw.

Ahead of us, Monsieur suddenly yanked his Peugeot off the road into a hidden laneway, and stopped. We could see below us for the first time the tiled roof of a little house. We stopped the car behind his and got out. The sky was blue, and the air was still and acrid with the smells of thyme and rosemary growing wild. We could see the vineyards and the trees and the mountains from the side of the little house. And hanging over us was an incredible, magic quiet.

We followed Monsieur Barruol through a stone archway and into the front yard of the house. He took us to the edge of the grass, where the hedge was growing by the wall, and showed us the tiny stream that chuckled through the front yard, pushing its way through the rocks.

The house faced south, and looked out at a small pine-covered mountain which rose immediately and abruptly on the other side of the stream. To the east, there were vineyards heavy with rich purple grapes, and a special personal row of grapes planted against the yard for the use of the tenants. There was also a small cabin with a roof made out of the same antique tiles as those on the house. It contained garden tools and firewood and had two large windows facing south. We could see that it would be a good place to hang clothes on a rainy day.

To the west, there was only wilderness and a Roman basin, and an unspoiled forested valley for the stream to run through. But if you walked down the road a few paces from the mailbox and looked west, you could see the lush plains by the Rhône, and the low mountains beyond.

And to the north, the direction that the prevailing Mistral wind comes from, the house was completely protected. It was built right into the side of a shallow cliff, and any wind that might come along would skim right over the house without even touching the roof. If you walked along the road, in other words, your feet were about level with the chimneys.

Monsieur took a large iron key out of his pocket, opened the front door of the house, and stepped in. It was completely dark and cool inside with all the shutters closed. We listened to him fumbling for a moment in the dark with a shutter, and then he opened it, and filled the entrance to the living-room with sunlight.

The entire wall on the opposite side of the room from the window was panelled with pine, and with the shutter open, it glowed warmly in a spotlight of sun. Monsieur went along the room, opening other shutters, revealing the rest of the room little by little, waking it up, bringing it back to life. An immense Provençal fireplace filled one corner right to the ceiling, with pot hooks and black iron pots and an oak mantel. And over the mantel was an antique double-barrelled shotgun. The floors were paved in red tile, and the front walls were made of stone, three feet thick. In the centre of the room was a splendid old table surrounded by stiff, rush-seated chairs, and behind the table stood a giant of a sideboard, looking darkly Spanish. But the dominating feature was the pine staircase angling up to the second floor.

We followed Monsieur Barruol up the stairs and inspected the two pine-panelled bedrooms with enormous lumpy beds and marble topped dressers. In one bedroom a side table was inlaid with many-coloured woods in intricate patterns.

We inspected the kitchen with its gas stove and refrigerator. We looked at the water heater, the shower, the bathroom and the water closet. We were very excited.

I nudged Lorna once. She nudged me back. We both wanted the house very badly. Our house. Our own house. All by itself in the countryside.

"Ask him about the rent," Lorna said very quickly in English. "It couldn't be right. There must be some mistake."

The guide book had said $120 a month. I was almost afraid to ask the question for fear of being disappointed. I remembered the little flat we had had in Toronto. It was a second floor walk-up in a bad neighbourhood, and we had to share the bathroom, and of course it wasn't furnished. We thought we did well indeed to get it for $115 a month. This place was furnished right down to the last garlic crusher.

"And Monsieur," I said finally, "What about the rent?" We both held our breaths. We prayed. We crossed our fingers and our toes. We would have paid anything he asked for the house at that point.

"It is $30 a week, or $120 a month. Whichever you want," he shrugged.

We both breathed out at once, almost collapsing into each other's arms, but instead managing somehow to look cool. "All right, Monsieur. We'll take it for a week. And then we will decide whether we'll stay longer."

"That's fine with me," he said. "Do what you wish." He handed me the big iron key.

"I'll come by this afternoon and pay you the rent. After I've cashed a cheque."

"Oh, no hurry." He started out the door. "Pay me when you want. Tomorrow. The next day," he called over his shoulder. "This is Provence. And in Provence, there is always time." And a moment or two later, he was off. Looking very disinterested in the whole matter. Hurrying back to his lunch. And we were left in the vineyards and the Dentelles and the silence, with our own house. We had rented it. It was as simple as that.

7

All over the village of Gigondas there were basins. Deep, concrete basins with slippery sides from centuries of soap, and filled with dark, green water. As clear as if it weren't there at all. To see a wooden bucket floating in the water was a mystical experience. It would seem suspended, green and motionless in nothing. Or entrapped in a sheer block of plastic.

"The sun is our life here," said Monsieur Jourdanet, who was an old man sitting on the bench in the square. "But water is the means." And everywhere we walked when we explored Gigondas for the first time, we could hear the water. It gurgled in the main square, it tumbled below the walls, we saw a little girl hoist another little girl up to a spout in the haute ville. We saw her drink with her throat moving, feeling the cool green liquid in the hot afternoon sun.

Most of the streets were very narrow in Gigondas. Too narrow for a car. We had to park the car in the square by Monsieur Jourdanet's bench in order to see the town. And when we struggled up the winding streets, and got above the place, every step was like going back in time. Back to the days before there were cars. Even to the days before carriages were common. The streets were so narrow. No one had even thought about carriages.

The bakery where we had asked directions was run by Monsieur Galon. The bread was hard and good. And Monsieur Galon pulled it from the ovens on long-handled wooden paddles. His face was lined and floured. He wore a beret indoors and out. At all times. Madame Galon ran the cash register, counting out the change in old francs, perpetually dressed in black. She was a large, kindly woman with curly grey hair. Their son, Jacques, who was about ten years older than we were, made deliveries in a Renault truck. Rural customers of the Gigondas bakery were treated unusually well, since a bread delivery service in that area was very rare.

Unlike most bakeries in France, the Gigondas one refused to bake early. Villagers complained and muttered angrily about this heresy, but Monsieur and Madame Galon were tired of getting up before dawn to service their few customers. If you ran out of bread before breakfast, you would have to drive over to Sablet to get a hot fresh loaf. Otherwise, you would have to buy a day-old loaf from Madame. One day a week, Madame Galon's sister would come in to spell her off at the cash register, and on that day, Madame would do her laundry in the stone basin by the Mairie. You could see her there in the morning.

From the street, we could hear the people talking and living in their houses. Sometimes the windows would be open, and we could see in. Other times, they would hear our footsteps on the stones, and bend out into the sunlight to see who was coming.

Past the bakery and on the same side of the road was the only grocery store in all of Gigondas. It was run by the stony-faced Madame Ughetto. We were frightened of her at first for she never smiled, and seemed to treat us with unwarranted hostility. Her groceries were also expensive; so for a long time we didn't go there often. But when her husband was home, or when her dark-skinned, five-year old boy came in the door, her leather face cracked into the most beautiful smile in town. And when she smiled she became a different person. Eventually, we made friends and talked about the cherry blossoms.

We studied the walls in the lower town. There was plenty of time. We saw how ancient doorways had been bricked in, or torn out, or remodeled, or cut in half, or made into windows. We saw some walls that seemed to be made up entirely of doorways bricked in from other times. Perhaps each generation of wives had different ideas about where the door should be, and each husband felt he could improve on the entrance to his courtyard. We weren't sure.

Sometimes we would meet Monsieur Granier on the street, pedalling past. He was the garde champêtre, the chief of police, the town constable. He was not much older than we were, and very handsome. His sole concession to an official police uniform was a gendarme hat. Otherwise, he wore a sweatshirt and rough work pants. Twice, he wore his full uniform. Once, when the television company came down from Paris, with their slick Parisian accents, and trailer trucks full of cameras and lights. They wanted to use Gigondas as a background for a story set a hundred years ago. They wore sunglasses, and woolly coats, and said clever things, and everybody got rather tired of them eventually. But for the first few days, Monsieur Granier was decked out in his entire uniform, looking like the chief constable in a fashionable Paris arrondisement. His shoes were shined to perfection, he had shaved, and he held back the crowds of spectators with superb stylish gestures. The only other time he wore his uniform was on Christmas day.

At the top of the town, above the grapes and gardens and the tiled and dusty roofs of the other buildings, was the church. It was a hard climb for the older people in the village, but the view from the churchyard was well worth the trouble. Someone told us that on a clear day when the sky was just right, usually on a day after the Mistral had come, you could see all the way to the Pyrenees.

The first few times we went to see the church, it was locked. So we had to admire it from the outside only. It was typically Provençal, with its curving plaster walls and wrought-iron belfry. The roof, all of red tile, was crimped up and down like marzipan, and fell together in impossible angles.

There was a path beside the church that went higher still, and we followed it up to the Old Town, where the walls that were built in the Middle Ages were still standing. We walked down a narrow ruined street, climbed inside a stone turret, and picked our way through the rubble at the base of a series of ancient arches. We sat in the shade of an arch and looked out onto the Plain de Soleil where it stretches to the Rhône. On another trip, we took water colours along and painted scratchy amateur landscapes.

From the northern edge of the ruins, we could see the paved road that twisted up through the vineyards from the Domaine de St. Cosme to our own house. From there we knew the road became quite steep and even narrower as it crawled a final kilometer to the Hôtel des Florets. As far as we knew, we were the only house on the road.

But when we tried the hill in the car one day, we noticed a tiny plastered cabin tucked behind the low scrub and wild pomegranates. As we passed, one of the mysterious "hippies" whom we had often seen on the road in front of St. Cosme poked his shaggy head out the door and waved to us—we had found out at last where he lived.

And when we got to the Hôtel des Florets, we found that the

road didn't stop there at all. It narrowed still further, and the pavement ended, but it continued almost unnoticed through the pines, and up a very steep climb. We took the road. We nursed the car over the rougher spots where rocks had smashed down the mountainside or where heavy rains had washed parts of the road right out. We bounced and jiggled around turns, avoided a pine tree that had fallen part way into our path, and suddenly came out into the open again, much higher up. We were completely alone.

Below us, the green slopes and vineyards nestled in the Germanic valley where our house was, although we couldn't see the house. The Hôtel des Florets pushed through the pines looking positively Bavarian. Up above us, the road still continued, winding up at a ridiculous angle at the very feet of the Dentelles.

We climbed again, hugging the inside of the road next to the mountain, afraid to drive on the proper side for fear of sliding off. There were no guard rails. There seemed to be no guarantee that the entire road might not just crash down the side of the mountain and disappear. It was just a horizontal slash in a gravel slide at that point.

Finally the road levelled off, and we went around in front of the Dentelles, and then behind them, all the time looking out roughly southwest, enjoying the same spectacular view that we had from the churchyard in Gigondas, but much higher up.

Eventually we came to a cruel stone tower that defied all laws of logic, engineering and balance, simply because it was standing. It was a perfect fortress, built on top of a sheer pinnacle of rock. Two lesser natural towers jutted out on either side of it, and a smaller man-made tower was set below it. We later learned that this impossible structure had been built by the Saracens. It had resisted the frightening Mistrals and the cold and the rain for centuries.

The day we climbed the tower the Mistral was shrieking, spreading our coats like sails. The wild olive trees were clutching at the rocks with dark roots like talons. We were afraid of being blown over the side. But the view was perfect all around us. We could see more villages and towns below us than we could possibly count. We decided that we could see a hundred miles. We thought we could see the sea.

Most of the time, those first few weeks were really hot with no wind: just like the summer time. For days and days no cloud would appear to break the searing blue monotony. At times like that, we picnicked in our front yard in the sun, or across on the other side of the stream, facing the house. I could reach over the edge of the picnic blanket and pick wild spices. Just anywhere. And add the taste of Provence to whatever we happened to be eating.

Our house was better than we could possibly have hoped. Every night, I would close all the shutters downstairs in the proper French manner, making them fast with the heavy iron hooks until we were shut in like a fortress. If we left the bedroom shutters open upstairs, we could hear the steady noises of the creek all night. And in the morning we could look out from our bed to the wooded hillside rising almost vertically on the other side of the stream, and see the light of the morning sun descending from the mountain tops, casting long slanting shadows.

We had no trouble with the facilities. Everything worked, and the kitchen was equipped for even the most elaborate meals. All we had to do was buy the groceries. When the house was first opened, we had to deal with a plague of extraordinarily long centipedes, and I was kept busy banging scorpions on the heads with a coal scuttle and tossing them out the window. But within a week, our house was virtually free of bugs.

Sometimes, if the evenings were cool, we laid a fire in our corner fireplace, using the stumps and branches from century-old grape vines. If we stayed up late for supper, we roasted potatoes and chestnuts in the coals.

We could sit on the striped blanket in the yard on those hot days when we really didn't feel like doing anything else, and read aloud to each other, or watch the lizards playing on the front wall in the sun, or study a scorpion scuttling under the shutters. There would be five long months before the baby would come, and time unfolded for us alive and richly detailed like a painting.

8

The Vaucluse was for us a shopper's paradise. Gone forever were our supermarket days: flying trips through fluorescent behemoths once a week; snapping up frozen meats and vegetables and another box of laundry soap; pushing past the bored gum-chewing check-out girl who never looked me in the eye. Supermarkets certainly existed in the south. The "Sumas" were the coming thing, in fact, in the larger towns. But we had discovered rows of tiny two-man shops on every commercial street in every village. And each store seemed to be run by personable, attentive shopkeepers; all selling nothing but the finest in quality foodstuffs. The fastidious French would never settle for anything less in any case. People we knew from Paris stocked up on mountains of groceries whenever they ventured south. We soon learned to shop as the French do: picking discriminately over a bin of tomatoes, sniffing and prodding the cheeses, buying one egg, or a half a loaf of bread. Whatever we needed for the meal ahead.

We liked to drive into Aubignan, which is just south of Gigondas, and do our shopping there once a day. We felt terribly European. Our own village's bakery and grocery store supplied most of the 750 citizens with their daily food. But we preferred the far greater variety and choice of the larger villages to the north and south. Because we didn't have money for travelling, every trip into town for groceries was considered an outing of major importance. We tried to explore a little each day and learn what we could about our new home.

There was no doubt about it: Aubignan was our favourite. We could always park the car right across the street from the squat, colourful row of shops. We could hear the bell in the tower along the wall ringing ten, and the succulent slap of laundry being washed in the stone, outdoor basin. Directly across the road from our parking place was a bird cage suspended from the wall, filled with multi-coloured tropical birds that we never knew the names of, and long-tailed ones that looked as if they might lose their balance and tip over backwards from the sheer weight of their plumage.

The café next door had several small tables squeezed onto the narrow sidewalk, and umbrellas that were never unfolded, and an owner who was permanently dressed in a scratchy red wool sweater and dark pants. Sometimes we would stop at the café for a morning coffee, or I would sit there by myself and let Lorna practise shopping in French while I had a drink with the patron.

"Are you tourists?" Monsieur Faury asked the first time we stopped there. "I have seen you in Aubignan before," he said, smoothing down his red sweater.

"No. We're not really tourists," I said. "We're living in Gigondas and . . . ."

"Ahhhh! Gigondas! Good! Good wine!" He made drinking gestures with his free hand.

We had never even heard of Gigondas until we found it in the Gîtes book. But we soon found out that everyone else in France knew all about it. Our village was famous for its wine, and every person we ever met in France invariably mentioned the Cru Réputé of Gigondas when we told them where we lived.

"Sit down, Monsieur le patron," I said. "You have no other customers, please be our guest."

Monsieur Faury scratched himself absently through his sweater and sat down. "It's a good day for going up Mont Ventoux," he said. "It's so clear."

"We haven't been up Mont Ventoux yet. We've only been in our little house three weeks."

"What?" He sat up in his chair. "Been here three weeks and not been up Ventoux? But you must! It's fantastic. Today is just the day. Just go out of here, and turn at Beaumes-de-Venise, go through Lafare and Suzette, then cross over at Suzette to Malaucène and then . . . up you go! This is my special route. Very pittoresque!"

"I don't know if we have time today. . . ."

"But there is always time. You are in Provence." He stood up suddenly. "Wait right here." He dashed into the café. A moment later he returned with a large map, a slight tear at each of the four corners. "Here. Here is the map off my wall. See the route you must take? Beaumes, Lafare, Suzette—ahh, what a drive! Malaucène, and then . . . up! You see? It's so simple."

"And today is a good day?"

"Good? Why it's perfect. When it's this clear, you can see for a hundred kilometers. Or even much more. But here, take the map. I don't want you to get lost."

"But it's right off your wall. . . ."

"What good is it doing there? Everyone around here knows all these roads anyway. Take the map and go up Mont Ventoux."

Monsieur Faury's advice was very good. Not only did we climb Mont Ventoux that day, but we went up many times during the next few months to find spices that grow in higher altitudes. Following the road that's closed once a year for racing cars—"CAUTION!" A highway sign warns. "Specially banked turns for racing cars ahead!"—we wound up through the trees, through the alpine meadows, to the summit where the climate is too inhospitable for any vegetation, and the wind never stops blowing. The road reaches the very pinnacle of the mountain, shouldering up beside the five-storey television tower and meteorological station. And the view is the most extended one in Europe. Monsieur Faury knew one of the drivers who raced up the hill personally: he was very proud of that fact.

Like the majority of grocery stores in France, the one two doors down from the café had all its fruits and vegetables displayed outside in copious bins. Over each bin was a miniature blackboard identifying the vegetable, telling the price per kilogram and the area of the country it came from. We liked to buy as much as we could from under the du pays blackboards, since that assured that whatever was being sold was locally grown and fresh, and usually cheap as well. We never bought more fruit or vegetables than we needed for the day. That way, their flavour was always superb. We found out that some classic French vegetables, like fine green beans, tended to be expensive —around 40¢ a pound. But other things like cauliflower or squash dropped to as little as a nickel a pound. As a rule, we could count on vegetables being fairly cheap. We ate a lot of them and kept our food costs down that way.

Lorna liked the French scales better than Canadian ones. She said that because everything was weighed in kilograms or fractions of kilograms, the weight was always divisible by ten. So she figured that when we bought small amounts, like two apples, or five carrots, we were much more fairly charged than we would have been in Ontario.

Madame Haud, the red-haired lady behind the grocery store counter, had a Provençal accent that clanged like a high-tensile steel plate being dropped on a concrete floor. She and her husband would chime out the ritual "Bonjour Monsieurdame!" whenever we came in the front door. Then all the customers who happened to be in the store, scrawny old ladies in black, young children, sallow men in slouching berets, would all turn around and echo, like something out of a comic opera, ". . . Monsieurdame!"

And we would have to answer, shyly and embarrassed at first, but in confident full song later, "Bonjour!" The ritual greeting took some getting used to. Even in post offices, a bunch of strangers lined up wordlessly at the stamp wicket would all turn and respectfully say their hellos and good-byes to us.

Inside the Aubignan grocery there were all sorts of cheeses. There was an infinite variety of pasta, a regional specialty; two or three kinds of canned soup, and always several unwrapped birds in the freezer. They were stacked like logs, feathers and all, on the frozen shrimp. A wild duck would be nestled up to a pheasant, both looking as if they'd been flash-frozen the moment they hit the ground. We used to watch the patron haul in half of a Gruyère cheese on his wobbly wheelbarrow, and hoist it laboriously up onto the counter. He would find his enormous steel carving knife with the wide flat blade, and cut us off a slice. We could see the steel blade moving down through the holes.

Although we found a lot of things very expensive, beer and wine were not. Even at a humble country grocery store, magnum bottles of Champagne, and very good white wines were stacked in impressive rows. But everybody drinks vin ordinaire with their regular daily cooking. The quart bottles are returnable, just like a pop bottle, and they're corked with plastic stoppers. After trying different types each day, we eventually found two or three brands that we really liked. The vin ordinaire of the south is nearly always red or rosé, always dry, sometimes harsh, but always perfect for Provençal meals. We never paid more than 30¢ a bottle for wine.

Beer was even cheaper, with the most popular brands running around 10¢ a quart. We liked the beer; it was golden brown, tart and very fresh. Often, when we were buying our groceries, we would see a small seven-year old boy shuffle in and pick up two quarts of beer, pushing the exact change onto the marble counter, and leaving without a word, while Madame Haud weighed the vegetables. He was hardly noticed.

But if vegetables and beer were a bargain, meat was not. The butcher shop right next door to the grocery store was run by the prettiest lady in Aubignan. Madame Lyon had blonde hair and blue eyes and a voice that cracked and went husky when she got excited. As soon as she spied the two Canadians coming towards the store, she would burst into peals of crackly laughter and be unable to speak half the time we were there.

We found it nearly impossible to tell what was on display on the shelves, because the ways of cutting meat in Europe are so different from in North America. To add to our initial difficulties, everything was weighed in kilograms and priced in francs, and there were all sorts of cuts and varieties of meat that were beyond my vocabulary. I had never shopped for meat in France before in my life. So we would stand in front of the counter, staring, fumbling through a mental dictionary, converting francs to dollars, customers awaiting their turn behind us, while Madame Lyon, in no hurry at all, held her sides from laughing.

I often remembered the plastic-coated packages of dazzling white meat labelled "chicken" in Canadian supermarkets. I never knew for sure what type of chicken I was buying, but sometimes I was positive that the bleached, eviscerated, frozen-thawed-sold-for-fresh drumsticks were lobbed off a thirty-year-old rooster. Yet in any French butcher store we ever tried, when we asked for chicken, they would immediately whack down on the cold marble counter a real CHICKEN! A big, plump, yellow-coloured *animal.* With feet and claws and a bright red comb, and horribly enough, a baleful eye staring up at us from the counter.

Rabbits came like that too—with great heads and eyes and curving teeth and furry feet. Sheer hunger eventually made me rather adept at home butchery, or whatever you call it. I would roll up my sleeves and close my eyes and hack away at the chicken awhile, and then wash it and dry it and salt it inside and out. But I would have to put it in the refrigerator for a meal or two to dissociate the bird from the gore.

When Lorna finally pulled it out of the oven, stuffed and golden and surrounded with juices, it would look rather like a Norman Rockwell Sunday dinner, and I could eat it without a moment's hesitation.

The flavour would always make it worthwhile. All our meat, and all our vegetables for that matter, had a flavour that we had never known before. In Provence, the flavour of everything seems especially pronounced. When you taste a rabbit, you can taste the white soil, the harsh blue sky, the violent colours, the rugged terrain, the acrid spices. You really taste.

Our last regular stop in Aubignan was the bakery. It was a miniscule out-of-the-way place, hidden down an alley lined with sleeping cats. But by the time you got halfway down the alley, you could smell the warm bread smells and the aroma of freshly roasted coffee. Honey bees would be bouncing off the window panes on the inside, and skimming the fresh delicate pastries on the special days. If you got there early enough, the bases of the panes would still be webbed with steam from the baking.

"What kind of bread is that?" Lorna asked, pointing to a puffy row of loaves snuggled up against the rock-hard baguettes.

"Milk bread," purred the sexily upholstered bakery girl.

"What's it for?"

Claudette snatched a hot loaf off the rack and thumped it down on the counter. "Take one home and try it. It is to eat. Just like regular bread, only different."

"How much is it?" Lorna asked timidly.

"Nothing. It is a gift." She smiled.

"But I must pay. . . ."

"Nonsense." She threw her arms into the air. "What's a loaf of bread? Try it!"

On another occasion, some plump unfamiliar-looking buns were lying in a basket on the floor, cooling from the oven. I asked Claudette what they were.

"They're chocolate buns," she said.

I looked at them, sceptically. They looked like plain, plump buns, or little loaves of bread to me. I thought I must have misunderstood. "Did you say those were chocolate buns? How can they be? They look plain."

"Certainly they're chocolate buns." She replied. "Look." She reached down and grabbed a bun from the basket and tore it in half, throwing one half dramatically over her shoulder, not caring where it landed. "Chocolate."

I looked, and indeed it really was hollowed out and filled with chocolate. "I'll take two," I said.

She reached for two steaming buns from the basket, gave them to me, and flung the torn half of the first bun out the door to a scratchy brown dog. I tucked my long loaf under my arm, and carried the two buns in a little package back to the car.

9

Other places may have elaborate holiday celebrations, and people may flood in from miles around for a famous fair. But in Gigondas, the only event of any importance in any given year is the vendange. All through the grape-growing region, the commencement of the grape harvest has always been a time for celebration. In every town, in every village, the same small circuses and the same tired acts plod up and down the chalky countryside with their wagons, spurring on the celebrations, just as they have for nearly a thousand years.

For weeks before the start of the vendange in the villages around Gigondas, we saw posters plastered on every available tree, building and wall, announcing the arrivals of the circuses. Tinselled orchestras were promised in the larger towns, and dancing in the streets at night when it was cool, under the coloured lanterns in the plane trees. And a Miss Vendange would be chosen out of the two or three possibilities in each village.

The banks had their special Vendange Hours posted on the doors, and the cafés were often open at different hours. When we drove in to the grocery store in Aubignan one day, we were the only customers. "It's very quiet in here today," I said.

"Oui, Monsieur," said Madame Haud from behind the counter. "The vendange has started in some of the villages. There will be few people in here for the next few days."

When we drove along the roads between Gigondas and Vaison-la-Romaine, we saw sun-darkened men out in the fields, feeling the soil, tasting the grapes, squinting up at the sky, waiting for the precise moment for their personal vendange to begin. The exact moment was a very important one. Too soon or too late would be a disaster.

And it wasn't long before nearly all the farms on the Plan de Dieu were in action. We saw Spanish and Basque, Moroccan and French workers all gathered in the fields, bent over the vines, some workers wearing yellow slickers in the early morning to keep from staining their clothes. All of them gathering the dark grapes into wagons. We saw the wagons trundling slowly down the roads, their rubber tires bulging with the weight. Sometimes they were pulled by horses or mules, but more often by special tractors. When we approached one of the great wine houses in Gigondas, or one of the cooperatives in the other villages, the air would be heavy with a smell like a newly-drawn cork, and the roads would be stained purple.

We had decided the very first week that we should drink wine at least twice a day—with both lunch and dinner. We decided that since wine was so cheap in France, it would be hard to do without. Vin ordinaire, for instance, was usually cheaper to buy than water! I had said that if we couldn't drink wine twice a day, there was no reason to be in France anyway. Lorna agreed.

"But don't you think our own landlord, Monsieur Barruol, has wine to sell?" she asked.

"It's hard to say. Why?"

"Because if he does, it would only be proper that we buy our wine from him. After all, he is our patron."

"Perhaps you're right. But we don't even know if he's in the wine business."

"He must be," she said. "His whole farm is planted in grapes."

"Let's ask him then the next time we go into town. Even if he isn't in the business, he'll probably tell us where we can get some good wine."

"I think it would be a good idea."

The next morning, we locked our new little house and wound down the road to the much larger house of the Barruols. We nosed the car around the little crowd of long-haired kids who seemed to be permanently clustered along the road in front of the Barruols', and pulled into the laneway.

These kids were a mystery. We hadn't been able to figure out who they were or what they were doing in Gigondas, but we always saw them on the road, wearing far-out clothes and coloured head bands, usually near the Domaine de St. Cosme, and they always waved at us. Perhaps because we were young and I had long hair like theirs. We half-planned to stop some time and make conversation.

Monsieur Barruol himself opened the front door of the house

on the first knock. "Pardon, Monsieur," I said. "I'm sorry to bother you at this busy time of the year." His yard was filled with workmen.

"I'm not busy." His arms were at his sides, and he looked at me patiently. "You won't bother me."

"We've been wondering whether you are in the wine business."

"Of course I am," he said. "In Gigondas there is no other business for a man who owns land."

"Then," said Lorna, "you must have wine to sell."

"But of course, Madame."

"Well, we've come to buy a bottle or two."

Monsieur le patron smiled kindly. "Entrez," he said. "Entrez then and let me show you my cellars. You must see the cellars to really know the wine."

We followed him through the open front door, down a long central hallway, and into an enormous dark basement that wasn't under the house, but behind it, carved into the hillside. It was very cool and damp.

Monsieur flicked on the light. We could see great black barrels lying on their sides in uniform rows. "Perhaps I should explain," he said. "You may find this interesting. The house here has been in my wife's family for a considerable length of time. It was actually left to the family by Mary Queen of Scots, just before she was executed. My wife's family is not French at all, you see. They are Scottish. That's how we ended up with this house. But they eventually changed their name to a French one." He turned and started walking down one of the corridors in the basement, his voice sounding hollow and damp. "But of course, these caves here and those out under the sheds are much older than that. These caves were dug by the Romans. They have been in daily use ever since."

We watched him take a small glass tube off a shelf, and climb a creaking wooden step or two beside one of the barrels. He removed the cork stopper from the top of the barrel, and pushed the glass tube down into the hole. When it was right down, he put his thumb over the end of it to trap the air and drew it back out, full and heavy with gleaming purple liquid.

He emptied the rod into a glass and handed it to us to try. The wine was cool and dark, harsh and strong, with a dry woody flavour. It was strange to me, but I liked it immediately.

"That's very good," I said. "Very different. Rich."

"Yes, very good."

He took the glass from Lorna and filled his mouth with the last of the liquid. He swirled it in his mouth and swallowed it. None of us spat on the floor or anything. "Young," he said. "Still very young. But not bad. Another year, and it will be good."

He led us over to a wine rack where there were perhaps 400 bottles lying on their sides. "How many did you want?" he asked.

"One," I said.

"Take two."

"How much are they?"

"Six francs a bottle, but one is a gift."

"Done!"

We both smiled, and I took the two dark green bottles. "We'll buy all our wine from you," Lorna said. "Every day."

"Oh no! That would be too expensive. Nobody does that. Not even me. I drink ordinary wine every day. This wine is for special occasions."

"Ah. I see."

"Drink it with a very good cheese, or with a heavy meal. It is not meant to be drunk alone," he said. "And if you want the flavour to be just right, it should be brought into the kitchen about three hours before you want to drink it, to warm it up. You should draw the cork then too. It will wake the wine up. Right now, you see, it is sleeping."

We stayed there for a moment, admiring the shape of the bottles and the very handsome label. It said "Gigondas. Domaine de St. Cosme." And there was a fine sketch of the eleventh century, Romanesque chapel that stood on the hill above us, and looked down on both the Domaine and on our own house.

"That's a beautiful label," I said.

"Yes. Not bad. I designed it myself."

"You? But that's fantastic! It's very well done. You have a real talent."

"Perhaps. I used to be a full-time sculptor and a cabinet-maker. What we call an artisan, or an ébéniste. But . . . ." He shrugged. "That was a long time ago."

He smiled again, and took us to the side door of the caves. We listened to our footsteps damply echoing. We stepped out into the inner courtyard of the house, blinking in the morning sunlight, hearing the ancient fountains shimmering in the yard. At the far end of the court near the arched entrance-way, a couple of workmen bustled back and forth from one building to another, struggling under a mountain of papers, rulers and odd pieces of equipment. There was a certain urgent look in their expressions. Monsieur le patron shouted out a few quick commands to the workers from where we stood by the fountains.

"You must forgive us for bothering you today, Monsieur," I said. "I can see you are very occupied now preparing for your vendange."

"The vendange? Oh no. I haven't time to think about that just now," he said.

"But what are your workmen so busy at then, may I ask?"

"Why, we're putting central heating in my house. It gets cold here in the winter, you know. This year I want to be ready!"

10

It was the third morning, cool and clear after the rain that our rural France cocoon was forever crumbled. I had read the telegram that the daughter of Monsieur le facteur had brought out to our house on her bicycle.

"It's a télégramme," she had said, bringing it out to where we were stacking firewood by the house. "All the way from Canada!"

"Ahh. Merci. Thank you for bringing it out to the house."

It was written on the familiar cheap blue P.T.T. paper, cabled from a friend of mine who was with a law firm in Ontario. "OCT. 12," it read, in large, scrawly penstrokes. "DECREE NISI GRANTED. DECREE ABSOLUTE EFFECTIVE FEB. 12. BETTER THAN NOTHING. JOHN."

"What does it say?" Lorna asked. "I don't understand." The imminent divorce case had been creeping uneasily into our minds for several weeks. Every day since the date for the case had passed, we had been expecting the news.

"Damn!" I said. "Damn damn damn damn."

"What does it mean?"

"Damn damn damn." I handed her the telegram. "It means we can't get married until the 12th of February. That's what it means."

"But the lawyers in Vancouver said everything would be all done in one day if we signed the papers they sent us. Remember? They said we'd be free to marry after that. What does this Decree Nisi mean anyway?"

"It means the lawyers bungled the case. A straightforward, clear-cut, uncontested divorce. With no money involved, and no children. It means the judge has granted you a divorce but . . . not quite."

"I still don't understand."

"Listen. You've been left in limbo. Neither fish nor fowl. The judge has given you four months in which you can change your mind and reconcile. He's giving you a chance to get back together before he makes your divorce final."

"But that's ridiculous. I don't want to reconcile. What about our baby?"

"Bungled," I said angrily. "The whole thing bungled. We should have been there." My father, who was a judge, had warned us that the judgement could come out the way it did. It seemed hardly possible at the time.

"What will we do now? Does the Decree Absolute come in automatically?"

"No. We'll have to make sure someone files for it on the 12th of February."

We both stood in the centre of the lawn, stunned. Watching the daughter of the postman peddle away around the last curve. Any plans for a late October wedding disappeared with her.

Lorna read the telegram again. "How do you know all these legal technicalities?"

"Dad told me." I sat down on the edge of the woodpile. "Listen. When's the baby supposed to be born?"

"You know that."

"No. I mean exactly. What day exactly?"

"Who can say! You can't tell things like that for sure. The doctor guessed about the last week in February."

"Damn! We'll be cutting it fine."

We were no longer isolated from the world. Canada thrust itself back into our consciousness. And the communications between France and Canada became frequent. We telephoned my father for his advice. We cabled Canadian lawyers. We talked to embassies. And eventually we began to get a clearer picture of our true situation.

The first thing we found out was that we couldn't have been married in France in October even if the divorce had gone through right on schedule! According to a fusty old French law, we could not be married until 300 days had passed after a divorce was final. Just to make absolutely *certain* that there was no possibility of reconciliation. Naturally, this 300-day waiting period was to be piled on top of the four months we were already having to wait according to a judge in Vancouver, B.C.

We ate up our savings on the telephone, finding out about the divorce laws in other countries. Switzerland, close by and a faint hope, turned out to be just as difficult as France to get married in. Belgium was out of the question. Ireland didn't know what a divorce was. That left England, where, it turned out, we could be married as quickly and as easily as we could have been in Canada after the 12th of February. The only complication was that we would have to be in the country fifteen days to classify as residents.

So we finally formulated a plan: using the last dregs of our savings, we would dash up to England on the night train. We would arrive there about February 1st, stay with friends as much as we could to cut down on hotel bills, put in the necessary fifteen days.

We calculated that the Decree Absolute would take about three days to arrive from Canada, so on or about the 15th of February, we would be able to slip out quietly and get married in whatever English church would do the ceremony in a hurry. And then, trying not to look too desperate, we would flash back to Gigondas by plane that very day, just in time to have the baby which would be due within two days.

It would all have to be done on a dead run without missing a beat, but we thought with careful planning, we could pull it off successfully. Over the period of the next two months, we dispatched letters to the law firm in Vancouver that had conducted the case, telling them where we would be on the day the Decree was granted so that they could forward us a copy to make things legal. Used to dealing with friendly Provençal businessmen by this time, who were attentive to our every whim, we were very much surprised when the Canadian firm didn't even bother to answer our letters. We were hopelessly frustrated.

Finally, on the telephone, my father kindly agreed to do something on our behalf. On his own, he hired a lawyer from yet *another* law firm who promised to make sure that the Decree Absolute was gained in time, and that we would receive it in England. And it was only then that we could attempt to put the case out of our minds again. At least until after Christmas. We tried hard to settle down again to enjoy our life together. To feel the baby blossoming.

My father thought our flying trip to England was a good idea. So did law firm number three, as they sharpened their pencils calculating our bill.

11

"There's only one way we can afford to stay here now," I said. "And that's to live on a budget, just like we did in Toronto."

"You hate budgets."

"Of course I hate budgets, but we weren't planning on running up all these intercontinental telephone calls. I'd sooner try to live on a budget than be forced to move out." I finished off the last of my breakfast coffee and took a final stab at the Provençal honey.

"I guess you're right." She scooped up the honey pot and set it on the tray. "We'll have to figure something out just to survive. Everything's so expensive here—a lot more expensive than you said it would be."

"Well, times have changed. It didn't use to be like this."

We cleared the table together, shaking the crumbs from the oil cloth out the door, and putting everything else from the breakfast away. Finally we found the pencils and paper, and pulled two stiff-backed chairs up to the table in the kitchen.

"Let's get this thing together then," I said. "What's our biggest expense other than rent?"

"Food."

"How much are we spending?"

"I don't know. We haven't been keeping track."

"Well, for a starter, let's set an arbitrary figure of $15 a week."

"No way. We'd never make it."

"How about $16 then?"

"You must be kidding," she said. "Food is murder. It costs more here than in Canada. Most things, anyway."

"What things?"

"Meat, for instance. Meat is murder."

"We'll have to cut down on meat then."

"Vegetables are cheap," she said. "We can eat more vegetables. And so is cheese. It's a meat substitute too."

"I'll go for eating more cheese," I said. "It's the best cheese in the world, as far as I'm concerned. What else is cheap?"

"Bread . . . wine . . . pasta."

"We can fill up on bread and pasta, and slosh it all down with wine!" I said, enthusiastically making notes.

"It sounds very French."

"The whole idea is definitely very French. There's nothing like being cheap." And we found out later, when we tried our budget, that we really could get by on $16 a week. We ended up changing whatever Canadian tastes and eating habits we had, and sliding unconsciously into the French ones.

We ate nothing out of cans. Everything had to be fresh; nothing was prewrapped or prepared or in plastic bags. Because we were careful, our diet became more nourishing, more varied, and we tried more things we hadn't tried before. Even better, we were never hungry, and we both lost weight.

"But if you ask me," Lorna said, "one of the biggest expenses has to be gasoline."

"Right on. It's bloody robbery. Somebody told me that it's the most expensive in the world. It's costing us $9 to fill up the tank of the Volkswagen now. And it's getting worse. I can hardly believe it."

"We'll have to budget that," she said, her pencil poised.

"But not too severely! We've got to explore! If we can't get around a bit, there isn't much sense in being here. We might as well take whatever money we have left and head back to Canada."

"How about $5 a week?"

"I'm hitchhiking back to Canada."

"Nine dollars then. One tankful."

". . . Okay, you're on."

Little by little we went over all our expenses. We pared everything down to the last cent. Cutting here, snipping away there, until we finally had a workable budget that we could live on if we were very careful, and still not do without.

"It all works fine, except for one thing," I said, pushing away from the table.

"What's that?"

"If we stick to this budget unfailingly, and if we follow it to the letter in every way, we'll be out of money in a month. Something's got to go."

"But everything already went," she said, thinking of the jazzy yellow dress in the window in Carpentras.

"The only thing left to cut down is the rent."

"But we're only paying $120 a month. That isn't exactly bad for a two-storey furnished house. Especially in an exotic spot like this."

"Too high," I said. "We'll have to see if we can cut it back."

"How can you say it's too high when it's so cheap?"

"It's too high for us. That's what makes it too high. If we can't get it lowered, we'll have to leave."

Lorna was quiet for a moment. Then she said softly: "If we can't get it lowered, let's not leave till we run out of money, okay? Let's not pack up defeated for Canada with money in our pockets."

"Of course not. We'll just have to leave sooner, that's all. Like in about a month."

"I'm glad you agree," she said. "Because I really do love it here. And if we can pull it off, I mean if we can get the rent lowered, and get married like we've planned, I'd still like to have our baby here."

For the second time in a week we headed down to the Domaine de St. Cosme. Again, when we turned in the driveway, we had to push our way through the crowd of long-haired kids at the corner. Again we parked the car by the fountain.

"Entrez, Monsieur," said Madame Barruol at the door. "Entrez, Madame." She led us in through the dark hallway that we had already seen, and off into a large room on the right. "Asseyez-vous, Monsieurdame. Sit down if you please. I will find my husband." She shut the door behind her, leaving us in the sitting-room. It was assumed that it was Monsieur Barruol whom we wanted to see. We hadn't yet opened our mouths.

We sat on prim, rush-seated chairs in the centre of the room, around a small circular table. After she had left the room we had a quick look around. Ornate military swords rested on the shelves to our right, surrounded by authentic flintlocks and ancient clay pipes and paintings on the walls. Beautiful classic furniture filled the room, with an exquisite inlaid table at one end as a pièce de résistance. I could see a very antique globe. There were leatherbound books with gold titles in a bookshelf that stretched from the floor to the ceiling, including a leather series on Plato. Some of the books looked very old.

"Good morning," said Monsieur le patron at the door.

"Good morning, Monsieur," I said. "We have been admiring all the beautiful things that you have here in this room."

". . . Oui. They're not so bad." He shrugged. "What do you think of my piano?"

"What piano?" It was a very big room.

"Right over here," he said. "Only it's not really a piano. It's a spinet. A very early one. It was around before Mozart even thought about his sonatas."

He showed us the small, square instrument in the corner, with a keyboard much shorter than a modern piano's. "It's completely restored," he said. "Better than new. I did it myself." He sat down on the stool and plinked out a few exploratory notes.

Lorna noticed a small stack of wooden flutes resting on top of the spinet. "Flutes," she said.

"Oui, Madame. Flutes. I play the flutes with my two oldest enfants. We play little trios together." He shrugged his shoulders and smiled. "A little Mozart, a little Rolling Stones. You know, the usual thing."

We all went back to the rush chairs and sat down. Madame Barruol arrived with Monsieur's cigarettes and set them on the table. Monsieur offered them around. I took one. I didn't even smoke. I was a bit nervous.

"Now," he said, as he lit my cigarette for me, "What can we do for you?" Madame sat forward on the edge of her chair, smiling.

"Monsieur, I'm afraid we have a bit of a problem."

"Oui?"

"It's about the rent."

"Oui, oui."

"Your rent is very reasonable, very reasonable indeed, and . . . I don't mind paying it a bit." I took a puff on the dark brown cigarette.

"Oui, oui."

"But we have made various calculations this morning, and have found that we just cannot afford to pay a rent that large for very long. We would like to stay here a long time, you see Monsieur, and be your tenants."

"Oui oui oui."

"I imagine, Monsieur that your little house will stand idle a fair amount at this time of the year if we are not in it. So I thought you might prefer to have some tenants living in there regularly, paying by the month, instead of having a tenant staying only a week now and then, but paying a slightly higher rent."

"Ah oui, I understand."

"Forgive me, Monsieur. I would not ask. I don't like to haggle about money, and as I've said, I think your house is well worth it. But . . . we simply can't afford it."

"Oui oui oui oui," Madame said.

They talked together unsmiling in a very rapid French patois I couldn't follow. The end of a beautifully budding friendship was in sight. When I thought of the ridiculously low $120 a month we were paying, I felt very badly. Like the world's worst penny-pincher.

"How does $80 a month strike you?"

"Too low."

"Non non non non. We would rather have you stay for a long time. As you say, the house is idle a lot at this time of the year, and you are reliable tenants."

"It's too low."

"Non. It's not too low."

I could feel the financial burden winging off my shoulders, making me feel giddy, light-headed, a happy customer straight out of Household Finance ad copy. ". . . Bon, Monsieurdame," I said. "If you are sure it is not too low, we will stay!"

"Ah bon!" said Madame. "We're very glad."

We got up and started for the door. "I'll pay you the rent for the first month on Wednesday."

"Oh, no hurry. When you have time. When you are around this way."

"We're really sorry to be a problem," I said at the door.

"Oh, no problem, no problem." He had already forgotten it. He squinted up at the sky from his doorstep and then down at his grapes. "Listen," he said, as if he were making his mind up right then. "Tomorrow I start my vendange."

"Your central heating is installed?"

"Yes. I have timed it well, don't you think? The grapes will be ready in the lower field tomorrow." I thought about his having to mastermind the whole harvest. Waiting for the precise moment when the grapes were truly at their peak, and then giving the order that would set all the wheels turning. There was no stopping once the vendange was under way. It seemed like a tremendous worry. My problems seemed so small.

"Those kids are gone," Lorna said in English.

I looked down to the end of the laneway for the familiar freaky cluster. "So they are." I turned back to le patron. "Monsieur, I sometimes suspect that you are running a commune here, you have so many hippies hanging about." I knew the provincial French liked to make jokes and tell stories about "les heepies." Anyone with long hair they called a heepie.

"What 'eepies?" he asked.

"The ones that are always standing around at the end of your laneway."

"Tiens! Curious, I've never noticed them."

"But they live just up the road from us. We have seen them."

"Where?"

"In a little white house on the left. Back off the road in the pomegranates."

"But those aren't 'eepies, Monsieur Brown! That's my house. Those are my sturdy workers!" He waved his arms expansively. "They're waiting for the start of the vendange!"

12

"Today's the day we're going to have horsemeat," I announced one morning very early.

"Horsemeat?"

"Horsemeat."

"You can't eat that. That's what they're always closing down Ontario restaurants for," Lorna said.

"Not any more. You can get horsemeat right in Toronto. It's a common thing."

"You're kidding."

"Besides, it's a great delicacy," I said. "Best roast beef I ever had came straight off a horse."

"When did you ever eat it?"

"Right here in 1968. I had horsemeat at a friend's house in the Nord. It was a roast: my friend's mother prepared it in an open pan in the oven. It was round like a log. I remember when we cut it open, the meat was dark and well done evenly all the way around the outside to a depth of about an inch, and after that it was rare. Really rare. The roast looked like a red bulls-eye on a target. My friend's mother had it just slightly seasoned with salt and pepper and very little else. Very subtle. And the meat was fantastic. It was really tender, and sweet, and fine-textured."

"But what did it taste like?"

"Like roast beef. I already said it was the best roast beef I ever ate. It was only when I complimented Madame on her choice of beef that she told me that it was horsemeat. Could have fooled me."

"Are you sure it was horsemeat?"

"Of course I am. Besides, an American friend of mine had roughly the same experience. He was stationed in Washington for a while during the war. He had a date with a girl he desperately wanted to impress, you see, and he had managed to land this date largely on the promise that he would arrive at her apartment with the largest steak she had ever seen."

"Then what?"

"Well, apparently at the time you couldn't get anything remotely resembling fresh meat in the entire city. But he happened to be a good friend of the butcher, and the butcher handed him an enormous horse steak under the counter. He assured him that the steak would be a great success. So my friend grilled it at the girl's apartment and was a tremendous hit. Until . . . later, when he was basking in the glow of good food, a bottle of wine, and the newly-found admiration of the girl, he made the mistake of telling her what she had been eating."

"What happened then?"

"She threw him out on his ear."

"I don't blame her."

"How can you say that? You've never tried horsemeat. It's a true culinary experience."

"I don't know. . . ."

When we drove into Carpentras later that day to do our shopping, Lorna watched for the daily bargains; I kept my eye open for a chevaline. In France, butcher shops are usually divided up into categories. There's the rôtisserie which has windows lined with colourful roasted meats, much like a New York delicatessen. And there's the boucherie, where you can buy beef, lamb, rabbit, chicken. The charcuterie is the place to shop for pork, bacon, sausage, and patés du porc. And finally, more or less at the bottom of the heap, there's the good old chevaline.

You can always tell a chevaline by the large, carved, blood-red horse's head hanging over the door. It is one of the few primitive signs left, needing no writing under it to tell you what is being sold inside. There can be no mistaking it.

The chevaline I found was spotlessly clean, and almost suspiciously austere, except for the rather dirty, unshaven man hulking behind the counter. While we were in the store sniffing and studying the various cuts of meat, little French housewives scuttled guiltily in and out like customers in a Yonge Street pornographic store. They looked quickly over their shoulders as they stepped in, almost as if they were expecting the long arm of the Morality Squad to whisk them off at any second. They spoke in hushed, embarrassed tones with the unshaven butcher, who immediately shouted back replies in VERY LOUD BROKEN FRENCH with an unidentifiable Latin accent. They were invariably taken aback. As were we.

Eventually, Monsieur the butcher turned to us and asked in his overpowering, loud, far-too-friendly way what we would like.

"We would like a nice piece of meat to roast," I said meekly.

"AHHH!!" he yelled, and after that I couldn't understand a word of his Latin torrent. The housewives who were standing in line for their meat behind us, eyed me wordlessly. Their turn was coming.

"To roast, eh? Good to roast, if you please."

"Si si si si!"

Lorna stared dubiously at the sombre red cuts lying on the dead white counter. Monsieur the butcher was hacking away enthusiastically at a piece of meat for us in the corner. Little bits of flesh flew into the air as he crashed down his great cleaver. I wondered how the store stayed so clean.

"Ask him how long we should roast it," she said. "There's no fat at all on it. It looks like it's liable to dry out if it stays in the oven too long."

"If you please, Monsieur, how long should this meat be roasted?"

"AHH!" he roared, in a flood of garlic. And again I didn't get a word. People behind me were beginning to shuffle impatiently.

"What did he say?"

"I haven't the faintest idea!" I said. "Just grab the meat, and let's get the hell out of here."

I paid for the parcel. It cost nearly as much as a decent roast of beef. I begrudged the price a bit, but as I had said, it would be an excellent culinary experience.

We carried the roast home in the car, sneaking looks at it now and then in the back seat, wishing it had been in a plain brown wrapper, waiting until we got home to really study it.

"It's not even marbled with fat," Lorna said. "It's just solid meat."

"Bloody good for you," I said, trying to resurrect my own enthusiasm as much as hers.

"Ugly colour too. Sort of a funereal red."

"You'll be able to spot horsemeat at a mile from now on," I said. "Don't worry, it'll look great when it's roasted."

Lorna sprinkled it with spices of Provence, salted it and peppered it, put a little olive oil into the pan, and roasted it carefully. "Just pretend it's a roast of beef," I called down from upstairs.

We had the horsemeat with steaming rice and green beans and whole roasted onions. We set the table with a nice bottle of Côtes du Ventoux for the occasion. Lorna brought the roast to the table plenty hot, with little brown puddles of meat juice swirling around the platter and the smell of spices in the air. We both stared at the meat in disappointment. It was about half the size it had been when it went into the oven. It had that cheap, opaque grey look to it that the very poorest sort of pot roast can have when it's roasted instead of disguised.

I set to work with the carving knife. It was marbled with gristle, and very difficult to cut. "Sometimes the first slice or two can be a little tricky," I said. And then I broke the knife in two.

"Poke around it with a fork and find a tender place," Lorna said. She handed me another knife. I poked, but couldn't find any other place where the fork would pierce it.

Lorna refused to even try it after that. And I never could figure out a way to cut it, but after some investigation, I found some bits that would give way. So I tore them off.

"It's really quite good," I said, making sounds like someone cracking walnuts with their teeth. "Nice flavour."

"I'll make a stew out of it," she said. "Boil the hell out of it. That'll make it tender." We both resolutely refused to admit that we were defeated.

So the next day, I hit the meat with a hammer for a while, and managed to cut it up into cubes with the help of another sharp knife and a pair of surgical scissors left over from Lorna's nursing-school days. And we boiled the hell out of it. Cooked it most of the day, and served it steaming hot again that evening in a lovely Provençal stew.

That evening, I broke another knife.

13

It was the afternoon of the seventh day of le patron's vendange when we knocked again on the great front door of the Domaine de St. Cosme. It was a grey afternoon, and the Dentelles were shrouded with haze. What sun we saw burst out periodically in long, translucent rays that extended down to the fields where the vendangeurs were working. We saw them on our way down, bent over the vines, not looking up as we passed, filling the narrow wagon behind the tractor with dark, heavy grapes.

We had promised to come by the Domaine at three o'clock to pick up Madame Barruol for her second English lesson. She had come once already to our little house, and she had taught Lorna some French while Lorna taught her some English. We had sat around the table in the living-room, drinking pernod, reading to each other with some amusement from an English textbook that Madame had borrowed from one of her children. Lorna found some recipes in a French magazine, and she and Madame painstakingly translated them into English.

"I'm terribly sorry, but I can't come this time," said Madame Barruol at the front door. "We'll have to put the lessons off for another day."

"But of course, Madame. As you wish."

Her crackling hair was pushed back under a kerchief. And as she talked, she pulled on a faded blue jacket, and a pair of gardening gloves. "Please forgive the way I look," she said. "But it is the vendange. . . . There is a little trouble."

"Oh?"

"Yes. As you can see, the sky is quite grey. My husband is afraid that it might rain, so I am going to help him for a while with the harvest." She tucked a non-existent black hair back under her pale orange kerchief. ". . . It's not the sort of thing I usually do."

"Of course not," I replied. I was sure it wasn't.

"But when the weather looks bad, we must all pitch in. If it rains, you see, the grapes will lose some of their quality, and some of their alcoholic content. And it is largely for the high alcoholic content that Gigondas wine is famous."

"Ah!"

"You must let us help," Lorna said in English. She was understanding French better each day, but was still talking in English.

"If you wish," Madame said. It seemed to please her that we would volunteer to help in this minor crisis. At least there was no hesitation in accepting Lorna's offer. "But you must go home and change," she said. "You can't work in your good clothes."

"We'll go home then," I said. "We'll be back in a few minutes."

"Are you sure you don't mind?"

"We don't mind at all. It'll be an experience."

"The field is an important one," she added.

"Of course. We'll be right back."

"All right then. I'll go over to the vineyard now. My husband is waiting. I'll see that my little boy Michel is here in the courtyard for your return. He'll lead you over to the vendangeurs."

We went home quickly, excited by the adventure and threw on our "bleu-jeans" and our oldest shoes. Following Madame Barruol's advice, we took off our sweaters and put them away. "Sweaters catch on the vines," she had said.

Everyone has his job during the vendange. Even the two oldest children of the Barruols, Michel and Monique, had to help out when they were home from boarding school. Michel was waiting for us in the laneway as we drove in, wearing a little patterned sweater and short pants. We could see Monique, black-haired like her mother, sitting on the doorstep surrounded by at least a dozen children. Monique was the eldest —nearly a teenager—and the children were her responsibility while Maman was in the field. They were the children of the vendangeurs, and were traditionally in the care of Madame when she was home. Husbands and wives were busy, working side by side all day on the vines.

We followed Michel across the road, and down into the important field. Madame Barruol smiled when she saw us coming, and put down her work and came to meet us.

"We're short of buckets," she said. "I am afraid you both will have to share one."

"Fine," I said. About twenty-five heads and shoulders popped up around the vines as we talked and looked at us curiously, or smiled in recognition. All twenty-five seemed tanned and healthy.

"I have found some shears for each of you." She handed us clippers that were like spring-loaded pliers, or pruning shears. "Now you have to be very careful indeed with these shears," she said. "They are extremely sharp."

"Okay. How do we cut the grapes?"

"Well, because you must share a bucket, you can both work on a particular vine together. It's really very simple," she said. "Just take the bunch of grapes in the left hand. Like this, see? Hold the entire bunch gently from the base. Don't grab it by the stem. And then, holding the shears in the right hand, and always right side up, you can snip the stem."

"I see." I could feel some of the workers staring at us over the vines. God knows what they were thinking. Probably that we were rich tourists just out in the field for a lark. They undoubtedly figured we'd cash it in after a few minutes and go home.

"But you must be sure, Monsieur, that your fingers are well out of the way before you snip. The shears are sharp."

"Of course."

We started then. Working together on one bush. Dropping the grapes gently into the bucket. The air was still, and no one talked. Everywhere around us, we could hear the sound of the shears—snip, clip, snip. If I had felt self-conscious before we started, I now immediately felt like one of the little community. Just as soon as I began to cut. We were all working on a simple common task, and there was a feeling of togetherness there in the vineyard.

Some of the friendlier "heepies" worked alongside us in a different row. They worked hard and fast, jumping earnestly from bush to bush, squatting down as they cut, their long hair hanging straight in the still air. The head heepie looked like one of the Rolling Stones. They were all tanned and tough and competent.

It was somehow reminiscent of the commune workers in New Mexico, watching the young vendangeurs. For some of them, this was a lot more than casual labour for spending-money. Some of them were intensely serious about the work, and knew a great deal about it. They discussed the various qualities of the grapes they encountered on the vine with le patron.

"Thirteen and a half degrees, wouldn't you say?" one remarked, tasting a grape off a particular bush.

"Non non," Monsieur would reply enthusiastically. "Fourteen degrees. At least."

Down at one corner of the group, a middle-aged man from Spain worked on his own. His beard was three days old, and his features were very dark. We heard that he had left his wife and family in their little home and had come by train, by bus, by hitching rides and by walking, all the way to do the harvest in France. He glowered at the bush as he picked. He couldn't speak more than a word or two of French.

Across on the other side of the group, by the two old ladies in their spotted kerchiefs, were the young painter and his wife. They worked side by side every year in the vendange. They lived close by and were friends of the patron. Every day, their little girl with the pale, wavy brown hair would wait for them at the Domaine. The young wife grinned up at us once as she worked, her sunburned nose peeling, and black eyes sparkling. The money from the harvest would help them through the year.

Standing on the seat of the tractor, overseeing everyone, was the foreman. He was a kind man. We had met him several times before. He was one of the year-round employees on the Domaine. But at this time of the year, when he had to keep his eye on a field full of workers, he was a little gruff, and he didn't smile so much. It was up to Monsieur to do the smiling.

Click, snip, click, snip, we were filling our first bucket. It was hard to see all the grapes on the bush. Sometimes I had to poke my head into the leaves ostrich-style, appraising the situation, looking for the odd little bunch that we had missed. Once, three or four grapes fell off a bunch that I was holding, and tumbled like purple marbles onto the chalk-white soil. Not worth picking up. Just three or four. There are so many. But later, when my back was almost turned, I saw Madame snatch them up from the ground and toss them into our bucket. There would be no waste.

We had picked four buckets and were starting on our fifth when Monsieur came by and tapped Lorna on the shoulder.

"Doucement, eh? Take it easy, Madame. You are carrying a little one, so you must be careful."

"It's not hard work," she said. Her hair was hanging dark and straight. Her brown eyes flashing like a gitane's—a gypsy's. She could have been born into a field like this one and working the vendange all her life.

"Yes yes, I know. But look"—he pointed to the sky—"the weather is changing. There is no need to hurry now."

The sun was poking out of the clouds again, sending long gold rays right down to the vineyards. He was right. The weather was changing. It was sort of classic, all of us working there. Biblical maybe. It reminded me of the pictures in the illustrated Bible stories they used to make us read in Sunday school. There were the same queer tones of green and pale blue. The same rays. God was undoubtedly sitting up on one of those clouds.

The mood was changing. People began to talk. Someone began to sing. Everyone joined in, singing an old song of the harvest, some singing all the words, others humming over the words they had forgotten or had never learned. Snip, click, snip.

"Where did you get that bucket?" I asked.

"I found it," Lorna replied.

"Madame Barruol said we had to share a bucket."

"I know, but this one was lying empty by a bush back there, so I took it."

"Well, be very careful with the grapes then. You must be gentle."

"I am being gentle."

I saw Monsieur climbing up the side of the wagon. It was nearly full to overflowing with grapes. He stood on the edge of the wagon, teetering for a moment, and then he jumped in feet first. He jumped up and down as hard as he could, packing the grapes into the wagon with his boots, trying to squeeze a last bucketful or two in. I wasn't so gentle after that.

Our hands were getting purple from cutting grapes. Not purple from the juice, but purple from the spray and the dusty yeast that was on each grape. Some bunches were mammoth. Larger than I had ever seen, heavy with enormous succulent jewels and so perfect that I thought I would have to take a picture of them if anyone were ever to believe me. Other bunches were small and puny. It depended a lot on the vine. Some of the vines were a hundred years old.

Out of the corner of my eye I saw Monsieur, still standing on the loaded wagon. His hands were at his sides, and he was very still, staring off into the sun and the clouds. Maybe he was thinking about catechism classes.

"Attention!" He suddenly shouted. "Attention, my workers!" He was still standing in the wagon, but with his arms outstretched. "Attention!" Everyone stopped, stood up and looked at him. ". . . You know? I was just thinking: it was the Europeans who discovered North America, wasn't it? It was the Spanish, the French and the English who began to settle there way back in the sixteenth century." Monsieur the historian. "And now," he shouted, "the Spanish, the French, the English, the Europeans and the North Americans—we are all reunited. Right here in my vineyard. Imagine that! . . . Think about that while you work."

Click, snip, snip, click. We bent over the vines again. Someone started to sing. I came to a vine that had white grapes on it instead of red. I looked over to see what I should do with them. Off to one side just at that moment, I could see one of the heepies eating a big white bunch. When he had a good mouthful, he threw the rest into the bucket. I did the same.

Later on, because I was concentrating on what I was doing, it was several minutes before I realized that a serious argument had started up. The foreman was shouting at the dark Spaniard. The Spaniard was scowling and grumbling grizzled Basque curses in reply. Voices were raised. Monsieur was called in to mediate, but could do nothing. The tall heepie who looked like one of the Stones tucked his clippers into his jacket and walked over to the wagon to help smooth tempers.

Other workers, including the man with the beard, shouted their opinions on the argument from where they worked. Soon they weren't working at all. And finally, as a last resort, Madame Barruol the interpreter, the only one who could really speak Spanish, was called into the centre of the squabble for assistance.

"What's it all about?" One of the workers ahead of me asked another. I listened carefully. His friend could understand a bit of Spanish.

"Oh, the foreman's calling the old Spaniard a lazy good-for-nothing dog. That's all."

"Why?"

"He says that the old one is just standing around doing nothing instead of picking grapes. And the Spaniard says it's not his fault. He claims he went up to take a pee in the bushes as soon as it was safe to do so—when the weather had changed—and when he came back, his bucket was gone. He's been stumbling around looking for it ever since, but he couldn't make anyone understand. He says he can't pick grapes without a bucket."

It hit me like a hammer. "Lorna!" I shouted. "Lorna! You've got that man's bucket." Anyone who was still working was stopped cold by the loud, flat English sounds. "Give him back his bucket!" My face was prickling red.

"But I found it!"

"Never mind that. It's his bucket, just give it back to him!"

And even after the missing pail was returned, and everything was explained, and the apologies went all round, the argument still raged on in that peculiar French way: going round and round, with everyone repeating his particular side over again, two or three times more. Circling around the core of the argument, attacking it with subtle, savouring finesse; each time with a slightly different phraseology, trying to make a whole from the sum of its parts. So unlike the blunt Teutonic, English method of going straight to the centre of a dispute and simply saying your piece, and leaving it at that.

As usual, no one would concede a single point. Some took the side of the Spaniard, some the side of the foreman. And everyone just kept talking until the whole thing petered out on its own, like a fire with no more wood thrown on it. Nobody ever won. All disputes like this one took place at high speed, which made them difficult for a foreigner to follow.

Lorna found out that it was not only because the language was unfamiliar that it sounded as if it were spoken so fast. The National Geographic Society said that American females can knock off an average of 175 syllables a minute when they talk. American males manage 150. But the indefatigable French of both sexes crank out 350 syllables a minute! And when they talk, it's like carving shapes.

When the sun was down and the sky was beginning to get grey and dusky, Monsieur Barruol climbed up once more onto the wagon and called a halt to the work. "It will be good again tomorrow," he said in his speech-making voice. "We are lucky this afternoon. Everything points to a good year. Finish the bush you are working on, and then go home to your dinners."

Everyone worked quickly on the last bushes. I pushed my head through the branches and looked about for any last grapes that might be hidden in the heavy leaves, or obscured by the dusk.

"Come over to the house as soon as you are finished," Monsieur whispered to me. "It is the hour of the apéritif."

"It will be a pleasure."

We walked up to the great house, carrying our clippers, feeling our tired backs, listening to the feet of the workers moving, watching the evening arrive. We washed our purple hands in the green, cool water of the fountain by the front door, and were taken into the living-room that we had been in before.

The painter and his wife had been invited too, and the four of us sat down around the little central table. The pale-haired daughter of the painter came in and kissed him and sat on his lap, and the five Barruol children tumbled in after her and shouted and played in the great room. Monsieur le patron climbed up from his caves carrying a special bottle crusted with age.

We all drank a little of the precious wine, the kind that can only be found in the house of a winemaker, and that is not for sale. The hour of the apéritif. A time for the family and friends. Monsieur and his two oldest enfants played a trio on their wooden flutes. The two children played soprano, and Monsieur alto. And when they were finished, we all clapped. Then the two children played several songs together, and le patron directed them with an imaginary baton, soothing them, coaching them over the more difficult parts, loving the music.

Then we all had drinks while Monique, the eldest, played some Mozart she had learned on the seventeenth-century spinet. We applauded again. Then Monsieur, with his drink in his hand sang a solo, leaning against the piano, eyes closed, letting his olive voice flow out of its own accord, as he mouthed the Latin syllables.

"I sang for ten years in the Vaison-la-Romaine choir," he said afterwards. We could all believe it.

The hour ended with a genuine swordfight, with genuine swords with sharp edges and points. The painter and Monsieur in a mock dispute snatched the antique swords from the shelves, and galloped up and down the room, fencing recklessly back and forth, shouting and thrashing, much to the delight of all the children. The blades flashed and smacked together, dangerously close to us all, but nobody could keep from cheering and laughing in approval.

The end of the day's work is always a good time to celebrate with your friends, especially when the vendange goes well. It is the hour before the very private family supper. We felt accepted and a part of the community then for the first time in that special hour. And outside, for anyone passing by in the darkness, the shutters were closed.

14

The sun, which was still a summer sun, was shrieking down on us the day we walked into town to the church. The yellow in the sloping plaster walls was bleached a blinding summer white, and we stopped for a moment, feeling the heat and the light. The front of the church was always a picture. To our left and below us, the Plan de Dieu was shrouded in haze, despite the heat.

While I was working in the early afternoon, Lorna had taken a walk by herself, and on her way home she had become caught up in the colours she had seen.

"Come on out!" she had shouted. She flung open the door and burst in on my work, all vibrant and smiling, full of the things she had discovered. "You've got to come down!"

"What for?"

"I want to take the watercolours and the brushes and climb up the hill and paint the church. I want you to come. We could sit over on that low little wall up there, and put the water bowl between us."

"Don't you think the light is too harsh?"

"It's the light of Provence, isn't it? It's the light that Vincent van Gogh raved about to Gauguin, isn't it?"

"I guess it is."

"It's a painter's light," she said. "All the colours are clearly visible. We may not be the greatest painters, but at least you can make visual notes for your stories."

We had taken the narrow path that we had found on the other side of the stream by our house. We climbed the steep, slippery bank, holding tightly to the branches of the scrub bushes to keep from sliding backwards. I carried the watercolour paper under my shirt. But when we got to the top of the bank, the path was easy. We padded along a tree-lined road that was almost wide enough for a car, and past some battered ruins that were so old and hidden that no one had bothered to identify them as far as we knew. Then we followed a winding black-top road that led us directly to the church.

It was a short cut. Our secret short cut. We could walk into Gigondas taking this route almost as fast as a person could drive on the road. We took it often.

"The door is open!"

"What door?"

"The door to the church. It's open," she said. "I can see from here that it is." We had tried it several times before in the past. It had always been locked.

"Let's go in then, and have a look."

As we climbed the white front steps, some laughing children unexpectedly splashed out of the opening as if they'd been thrown from a bucket. We waited quietly, mildly surprised until they had all gone by, and then stepped through the huge varnished door into the cool darkness.

"Visitors!" an enormous voice shouted immediately. "Visitors!"

Our eyes had not yet adjusted to the light or the climate indoors. The voice boomed out of the darkness, rich and full, brimming with life and enthusiasm. I heard the footsteps approaching long before I saw a figure materialize in the gloom.

"Welcome!" I could see the stiff white flash around his neck. "Welcome to my church!" He shook hands vigorously. We could see his face by then. He was big. Really big. And although he wasn't a young man, we could both tell by his handshake that he was immensely strong. Great clouds of fine white hair fell in separate strands around his bright red face as he talked. We both liked him immediately. "Are you tourists?" He could guess that from our clothes.

"In a way," I said. "But we live here now."

"Live here? But where?" He threw his arms up into the air in a vast questioning gesture.

"In a little place called Valbelle," I said. He was leaning forward, absorbing my accent, frowning a bit in concentration. His lips were moving, listening to every syllable I formed, soaking me in. "It's a house on the Route des Florets."

"AHHHH! La Route des Florets. Of course!" He threw his

arms into the air again with delight. "I know it!" He chuckled. "I know the place well!"

"We are staying there indefinitely."

"But this is fantastic! Where are you from? What country is your homeland? Are you German? I can speak some German!"

"No. We're from Canada."

"Ah! From Québec!"

"No. From Toronto. English Canada."

"Oh. I see. But that doesn't matter. Come and see my church."

Now that our eyes had adjusted to the almost total darkness, we could really see around. We could see, somewhat disappointedly, that it was quite plain and grey inside, and not nearly as interesting or traditional as it was on the outside. But while we were looking, the benches started filling up with people from the town. Most of them were old, and some were still puffing from the steep climb from the lower streets. We realized that although it was a weekday afternoon, Monsieur le curé was getting ready to say Mass.

"We must go," I said. "You are going to say Mass."

"Are you Catholique?"

"No. We are only a couple of Protestant heretics," I answered.

"Ah!" he laughed. "Good for you. Well said!" He laughed again. "But wait here for a while. There's still plenty of time before the service starts. Have a good look around." We were slightly embarrassed. The church was very poor, and there was very little to see.

A very old woman got up from her pew and crackled down the centre aisle to the back of the church. She was dressed entirely in black. Black shoes, black stockings, dress, sweater, black hat. She tugged at the puny grey rope that trailed up to the ceiling and disappeared through a hole. Immediately the bell in the wrought-iron tower outside began to ring. She kept on pulling while we talked, occasionally flicking impatient glances in our direction. Like a starling. She was one of the old order.

"Listen," said Monsieur. "You are fairly new here aren't you?"

"Yes." The bell kept clanging. "We've been here less than a month."

"Ah! Then I must take you on a tour! There are so many things just around your house. There are many curiosities."

"That would be splendid."

The bell stopped ringing, and the starling darted a look at Monsieur with a yellow eye, and strutted back to her bench. People began to shuffle restlessly in their pews. The organ started to play.

"Monsieur! Your Mass. . . ."

"Yes yes, I know." His voice echoed through the church. "But we can have an excellent time. I know some heepies on the route. You have long hair. I can introduce you!"

"Not the vendangeurs of Monsieur Barruol?"

"Non non non. Real heepies. They have wonderful posters in their house. Very clever. They say things like . . . oh . . . how does it go?" The organ was hinting louder and louder. "Make . . . love . . . not . . . war. That's it! 'Make Love Not War'! Not bad, eh?"

"No. Pretty clever." I looked at Lorna.

"Bon! I'll meet you at your house then." He suddenly dropped to a whisper. "Right after my Mass."

"Fine."

He turned around then, with the organ music rising to a crescendo, and as if he were taking off one cloak and putting on another, he strode right into his service and started droning out the familiar, serious words. We closed the great door as quietly as we could, and dropped the latch and left him to it.

The heat had not really penetrated the house when we got home. We had time to close the front shutters and rest in the kitchen where it was cool, and have a glass of wine. The sun blazed through the cracks left open for ventilation, and scorched hypnotic patterns on the floor. We were home nearly an hour before we saw a pale green Citroën Ami pull up into the lane. I went out to meet Monsieur as he ran down the steps.

"You are here!" he shouted. "I thought perhaps you might have forgotten!" He seemed more exuberant and full of life than ever.

"Of course we haven't forgotten. We've been sitting here waiting for you. You must be exhausted after your Mass, Monsieur."

"Not a bit. Not a bit." He grinned.

"Come in and have a glass of wine then. Before we set off on our tour."

Monsieur le curé squinted up at the sky. "No . . . there isn't time," he said. "I have to be back at Vacqueyras in the early evening. I have another Mass there, and some things to attend to. I have another church there, you see."

"Ah. I understand."

"Besides, we must go while the light is so good. It will be spectacular within half an hour."

"You're right."

He looked down the steps behind me. "Isn't Madame coming?"

"Yes. She's waiting for us in the house. I'll go tell her we must leave immediately."

"Good. And then you two can follow me in your Volkswagen, if you don't mind. We'll take the two cars. Like an army convoy. That way, when we get to Vacqueyras, you can come straight on home, and I won't have to come with you to fetch my car."

Monsieur le curé drove straight up the Route des Florets, up the same lonely road we had tried ourselves on several occasions now. Past the hotel, and past the Club Alpine de France which is jammed right up against the hotel, and looks as if it might be a part of it. The French climbing team trains in the Dentelles, and the peaks loom over their clubhouse like grey New York skyscrapers.

We tore up the narrow little gravel road that is a continuation of the Route, and followed the priest through the pines to the open space where there is a fork. The right hand road went on up to the Saracen tower. The left fork was a barely discernible goat trail of a road that we had just explored for the first time two days before.

Monsieur stopped his car at the fork and got out. "We are going to take the left fork here," he said. "It is a little known road. But very interesting."

"Good," I said.

"Have you ever seen this road before?"

"Well . . . yes. We were down it two days ago."

He threw up his hands in astonishment. "But what is the use? If you have already seen it. . . ."

"Non non, Monsieur. We have seen it, but we didn't have an expert guide along before. Someone to point out the fine points."

"Ahhhh! Good! Let's be off then."

We bumped along the tiny road, plunging through the rock slides and the open spaces, and all the time as we drove along, Monsieur was tooting his horn, waving his arms, flashing his lights, and pointing this way and that at the monumental natural sights that were on every side.

Finally, we began to climb again, up a very difficult and rutted road. Portions of it were washed out from heavy rains, and there were sharp pink boulders sitting right in the middle of the travelled part. Sometimes we were forced off onto the spongy shoulders until the trees and the broom plants were scratching at the doors.

"We're going to go by that old chapel that we spotted in the hills the other day," said Lorna. "Perhaps Monsieur knows about it."

As we rounded the bend on the edge of the cliff, Monsieur le curé ahead of us suddenly yanked his wheel, and jammed his car off into a precarious clump of olive trees. He motioned us to do likewise. And almost before his car had stopped, he was out of the door, and running back to our car.

"I want you to look high up on that hill," he said. "You see? Hidden away there in the olive trees and scrub. Way up there. There's an old stone wall showing. Do you see it?"

"Do you mean by the chapel?"

His eyes widened. "What? You know about the chapel too? But this is incredible. How?"

"I don't know. We just happened to see a piece of the roof through the trees the other day. So we stopped the car and climbed up to investigate. We took some pictures and. . . ."

"You have even been up there?"

"Well . . . yes."

"But this is incredible. Nobody knows about that chapel! You have the eyes of a predatory hawk." He threw his hands into the air, exasperated. "I can show you two nothing."

"I am sorry, Monsieur."

"No need to be sorry. But it is you who should be taking *me* on a tour." He sighed.

"Do you know anything about that chapel? We couldn't find anything about it anywhere."

"Yes," he said, brightening. "It was I who managed to get it restored. But now. . . ."

Lorna and I remembered the spectacular view from the front door of the little building. We could see all the way across the valley from there, and down into the main streets of the two hidden mountain villages on the other side. We had sat out on the only level place outside the door—a small, flat rock surrounded by wild olive trees. We had studied the vineyards far below us falling recklessly together and we had listened to the sounds that the wind made.

"It's very beautiful up there," I said.

"Yes. It is."

There was no laneway in to the house of the heepies. We had to abandon the cars on the edge of a sharp turn, and struggle down a steep thorny slope on foot, scratching a quarter of a mile through the spices to the front door. And when we got there, there was no one home.

"Curious," he said. "There are six of them living here. Usually there is someone here." There was a pen of ducks in the yard, and a white whiskered cat, and some yellow clothes hanging on the clothesline, but no heepies. "We'll have to come another time."

It seemed as if everyone we knew tried to get us to meet "des heepies." And if they didn't happen to know any ersatz acid heads, they at least knew someone somewhere who spoke English. "There is a lady who is English who lives in the little village of St. Didier," they would say. "My cousin knows her. It's only thirty-five miles; we must drive over and see her." All of our friends seemed to be dedicated to scouring the countryside for anyone who could mouth the English language, or who had hair longer than usual. There was no explaining that we could meet plenty of English-speaking people in Canada, and that it was the French we wanted to know.

Monsieur le curé plunged on down a tricky descent in his Citroën with us right behind him. Some of the corners were covered with deep sand, and so tight that our car could barely make them at 5 m.p.h. with the steering wheel cranked hard over. And every now and then, with the sun setting, Monsieur would jam on his brakes in the middle of the road, making us literally stand our V.W. on its nose to keep from hitting him. He would leap out of his car, his white hair wisping in the breeze, his florid smiling face looking redder still in the setting sun. He would run back to our car as we unrolled the windows, with his arms outstretched, pointing up at the high red cliffs, shouting "Quelle couleur! Quelle couleur!" And then he'd sprint back to his car and be off, in a shower of gravel.

Finally he pulled off the road once more at the base of a long, treacherous-looking gorge. There was a clearing by the road in some lime trees where we could park the cars, and above us a small green stream scratched its way through the rocks.

"I am sure you never stopped here," he said.

"Well . . . we . . . ."

"What? Encore? Here as well?"

"We stopped . . . but we didn't get out of the car here."

"Ahhh!" His face lit up. "Then you haven't climbed up along the banks of this stream?"

"No."

"At last!" He threw his arms into the air. "At last here is something I can show you! Come!"

He bolted off into the prickly underbrush, and then when he saw we weren't immediately behind him, he wheeled right around and poked his white head out of the bushes. "Come! There is a path. Look down by your feet. There are blaze marks on the rocks."

"Why so there are, Monsieur. We wouldn't have noticed them if you hadn't pointed them out."

"Is that right?" he asked sharply. "I'll have to repaint them soon in that case. They must be fading."

"You mean *you* painted those blaze marks?"

"Of course."

As we climbed, Lorna said that she had always wondered who the guy was who made the arrows or painted the blaze marks on things. She was quite fascinated to meet a mark-painter in the flesh. "It's sort of like meeting a celebrity."

As we straggled up the fairly difficult, steep sides of the gorge, Monsieur le curé told us proudly that he had been the one who had painted most of the amateurish little signs and arrows that we had seen in the area—signs that pointed out unknown roads and trails, and little-known curiosities that were well hidden in the garrigues. We also found out that he was very active in restoring and preserving all sorts of old ruins around his parish. "I have forty-two churches and chapels in my parish," he said. "So, as you can imagine, it keeps me busy."

Despite his great size and his red face, Monsieur climbed like a goat. He would leap ahead from rock to rock, and then double back and help Lorna through the tricky parts. "Take it easy, eh? Easy. No use slipping and falling." He had no idea that she was pregnant. He led us up about a hundred yards or more in vertical height above our cars until we finally came to a spectacular green waterfall. The water tumbled white about twenty feet into a rocky green pool. And because there wasn't much water, and it was a long way to fall, it was like rain when it landed. The water was a cloudy green. Not green like crystal. Lorna figured that it was probably miniscule clay particles that gave it the odd metallic colour.

The pool was perfect. It was large enough to paddle in—or to do soap commercials—and the water rested there awhile before it poured through a hole worn right through an immense yellow rock that must have once acted as a dam. And then the water fell again in another waterfall.

"Listen," said Monsieur, putting his hand to his ear. "So tranquil," he whispered. "So calm!"

When we had seen and heard enough, we followed him back down the trail. The climbing was even more difficult coming down than it had been going up. And the evening was really upon us.

When we got to the bottom of the gorge, we all stopped by the cars and looked back up at the sheer cliff walls. The rock lay in mammoth black and white stripes or striae, layer after layer, hundreds upon hundreds of them. There were places where the striae waved up and down in parallel bands like bacon. At one spot, all the stripes made a monumental right-angle turn and stood straight on end. The pressure there must have been tremendous.

High up, at the top of the gorge, where there were some olive trees growing, we saw a flare of orange from the sun. The very last rays. And they disappeared as we stood there.

"You know," the priest said, serious and quiet now, "I think we are all very lucky to be living here."

And we both agreed.

15

Vivid new sensations of sun-darkened people and their land coloured our every thought, but the worry over Lorna's divorce proceedings in Canada never really let go of us. It was always poking out of our subconscious. Just to keep in touch with our various Canadian experts required a steady flow of letters and calls. To make things happen required a plague of communication. As a result, we slowly came to know all the idiosyncrasies and eccentricities of our local post offices, and the French postal system in general. We became true connoisseurs of the P.T.T.–Poste, Télégraphe, Téléphone.

Since their inception, the French post offices have always rivalled the provincial art galleries and museums as bastions of local culture. Although most of them are done up modern on the outside in a uniform Fifth Republic yellow, they are all very different on the inside. Their interiors tend to reflect the standards and needs of their communities. They are the place to meet your neighbours and catch up on the gossip while you stand in line, or to see who is telephoning whom and for what. They are potentially one of the hotbeds of information for the privileged few.

Rumours were afoot that our postmaster in Gigondas was "nothing but a sale communiste." But it wasn't politics that kept us from mailing letters from Monsieur Joubert's cramped little office. It was his alarming habit of charging practically double what any other office in the area tended to charge for a letter posted to Canada. We never knew whether he was genuinely mistaken or not, but I always liked to pretend that the Partie Communiste Français was snapping up the benefits from our grizzled facteur.

His telephone rates, on the other hand, remained relatively constant. And since his office was just down the street, in between the bakery and the newspaper store, we used his telephone quite often to call friends in other villages.

"I would like to call number 24 in Séguret," I would say.

"Le numéro 24," Monsieur Joubert would answer. His blue eyes were glass-hard like a hawk's, his voice thorny and gruff. "Oui, Monsieur." He would record the number carefully in his daily log book.

Lorna and I would stand behind the counter and study the colourful posters urging us to enter any one of a dozen lotteries, or commit ourselves for life to an insurance policy with one company or another. All French post offices seemed to be festooned with lottery and insurance posters—the French must be a pack of gamblers.

"Le numéro 24." Monsieur would push the small silver lever on his telephone which would signal an operator in Orange that there was someone who wished to make a call. And then we would wait some more. Loud buzzes and hums and clicks would chatter out of the unwieldy office equipment. Through the open door behind the counter, we could smell cooking smells from the kitchen, and occasionally we would see Madame Joubert or her sexy young daughter scurrying past carrying a steaming pot.

Finally the returning ring would sound on the telephone, and Monsieur would grab up the receiver. "Hallo, Orange? The Post Office of Gigondas here. Le numéro 24 at Séguret, s'il vous plaît." His voice scratching out the words.

Then there would be another long wait, and more croaks and buzzes from the equipment. Monsieur would fix his impatient blue stare on something outside the window, and drum his long fingers on the desk, the receiver jammed tightly into his ear. And as the time passed Lorna and I would begin to edge towards the cramped soundproof booth. Suddenly, with a note of triumph in his voice, Monsieur would shout: "Hallo? Hallo! Le numéro 24 at Séguret? . . . Oui? Is it you? . . . Don't hang up. Ne quittez pas!" Once the connection was made, every second cost. Time was money. He would motion us frantically to the booth, and we would sprint across the slippery tile floor and jam into each other in the narrow doorway of the booth, forgetting whatever it was we were phoning about in the confusion. I would snatch up the receiver and toss the little extra earphone to Lorna.

To make matters more complicated, a great number of our

friends couldn't speak English at all. And they would be so excited about getting a call from the post office, and so worried that it would be costing us a great deal of money, that they would soar off in a literal torrent of French. We always found it much harder to understand French when we couldn't see lips moving and arms being expressively thrown about. But to make things worse, we would inevitably end up with a poor transmission with lots of static and faint voices, and we would have to "Hallo" back and forth interminably just to establish that we were both really on the line.

At the height of such confusion, there was an unexpected cue for Monsieur Granier, the chief of police, or Monsieur the mayor or somebody else of importance to burst into the office, and we would have to reach out the door and say our "bonjours" and shake hands.

The P.T.T. in Vaison-la-Romaine, on the other hand, proved to be a very good one for sending letters to out-of-the-way places on other continents. They were used to tourists there. They knew all the complicated charges, weights, and formalities for every sort of letter or telegram going abroad, and they could rapidly spit them out off the tops of their heads.

By some absurd governmental decision the duties of the office were unevenly divided between two men sitting side by side behind the counter. Vaison was a chronically understaffed, permanent madhouse. An endless line shuffled up to the one rumpled little man who worked at a fever pitch surrounded by a hopeless confusion of scales and papers. Like most postmen, he licked the stamps for you, and pounded them on with his fist. He weighed the parcels, he changed the money, and he ran the telephone all at the same time, while the other man sat baldheaded at his immaculate little desk and cracked his knuckles idly or watched the clients pushing in. We never could figure out what he did. The scene always amused us tremendously.

"Hallo? Le numéro 7 at Carpentras?" The rumpled man would shout. "Oui? . . . that'll be five francs, Madame. . . . Hold on! Don't quit the line! . . . Yes it costs more to send it there by air. . . . Hold the line. . . . Your call, Monsieur. . . . No you don't need an airmail sticker for that. Everything that goes there goes by air. . . . Use booth number three, Monsieur! . . . Thank you, Madame. . . . Oui oui I can change it. . . . HOLD THE LINE!"

While standing in line one day, I noticed a pair of excellent tranquil watercolours hanging on the wall behind the two men. Paintings of quiet Provençal streets and trickling fountains. Someone had been a true artist. Everyone in the yellow office twitched impatiently in line, waiting for their turn to be caught up in the confusion, and in pleasant contrast on the wall were these lovely soft, summery scenes.

After having noticed the watercolours on several different occasions, I finally couldn't resist asking about them any longer. Rather than wade through the long slow line and bother the poor rumpled little postal worker any further, I purposely strode over to the second wicket and asked the name of the artist. Monsieur swivelled his bald head arrogantly away from the window. He crooked an imperious eyebrow and stopped cleaning his fingernails.

"I beg your pardon, Monsieur?" He was truly shocked that I should dare to interrupt him.

"I said, who painted those fine watercolours you have there on your wall?"

"I'm sorry, Monsieur. *I* can't answer that." He jerked his thumb in the direction of his beleaguered assistant. "You'll have to ask *him*! That's his department."

The little post office of Vacqueyras was on the way to two of our favourite shopping areas, and the ageing proprietors, Monsieur and Madame Gros, were both very careful with our mail. They always treated us like local celebrities as we dumped them with letters going all over the world.

"Ahhhh! Bonjour Monsieurdame from Canada," le facteur would say. "You are back again with more letters."

Madame Gros, who was his assistant would be seated with him behind the counter doing her afternoon knitting. As we came in she would tilt down her head and scowl over the tops of her glasses at us. At first we were rather put off by this frosty grey glare. But later on, we realized that she was merely pulling down her face muscles so that she could squint out over the tops of her glasses.

"Bonjour Monsieurdame," she would echo, and there would be much handshaking all round as I handed them our correspondence.

"Where are your letters going today?" Monsieur would pick up the first one and read the address. "Tiens tiens. Imagine that.

All the way to Canada." He'd throw it on the scale. Then he and his wife would watch transfixed as the needle rose up and swayed back and forth over the five gram mark. "Ohhhh! Almost," he would say. "It nearly passed over the five! You would have had to pay much more if it had." We would nod silently. We were well aware of it.

Two or three other people would file into the office while the weighing of each envelope went on. We would all nod at each other and murmur our bonjours. Occasionally some of the villagers whom we knew would come in, and then all weighing would have to stop while the conversation began. Once in a while, Monsieur le curé himself would burst in with a great pile of letters, and envelopes would be fluttering out of his hands like a snowstorm. When the curé arrived, there would be utter pandemonium.

"Now, let's see," Monsieur the postman would continue. "Under five grams . . . under five grams. . . ." He'd ponder for a minute. ". . . I'll have to look it up." We knew perfectly well what we'd have to pay on a letter, since we were spending nearly five dollars a week on mail. But there was no telling Monsieur. No matter how many times we dropped by a week, he'd still go through the same laborious ritual. There would never be any mistakes. Out would come his great black book with the green pages filled with charts and graphs and complicated lists and conditions. "Canada . . . Canada . . ." he would say, turning the pages. "Canada, Canada, Canadacanadacanada. Oh! Canadacanadacanada. Ahhhh! Here it is! CANADA!"

"Let me see it!" Madame Gros would say. She sharply double-checked everything he looked up. "Fifty centimes, Monsieur!"

Now Monsieur would pull out a second book, or perhaps consult his detailed chart on the wall. "Letters under five grams. Letters . . . letters . . . letters. Ahhh! LETTERS UNDER FIVE GRAMS! Here it is!"

"Where?" Madame Gros scowled over the top of her glasses.

"Here! Right here on the wall!"

"Forty centimes, Monsieur."

"Fifty and forty, fifty and forty, that's . . . NINETY CENTIMES!"

"Ninety," she would echo, and she would write it in the corner of the envelope.

Then they would weigh the next letter, and the next; and

then carefully count the number of words on a post card. If you wrote too many words, you had to pay more. Then, when we were all done, they would record all the figures on a scratch pad or scrap of paper and add them up, all the time double-checking on each other, and sometimes both of them would add if there was no one waiting.

Finally they would present me with the Grand Total. I would pay up while they dragged out their stamp books, and Lorna and I and Monsieur and Madame would all lick the stamps, and then Monsieur would ink up his heavy old brass canceller, and stamp the living daylights out of all our letters, making them look terribly important and official.

The tiny mountain village of Séguret had the only other post office we used with any regularity. The building was always spotless and interesting and filled with so many flowers that the windows were steamed up like a greenhouse. The bureau was run by a fascinating man called Monsieur Sias who was completely bald. Whenever we opened the door, he would shout out in delight, and literally fall all over us. He was a very kind man.

Hanging proudly on his wall behind one of the larger bits of jungle greenery was a framed certificate issued by the government—one of their highest honours. In flowing script, it stated that in a rigorous inspection of the entire region, the post office of Séguret had been judged, "The Most Coquette Post Office in all the Vaucluse!"

16

The sun pushed up from behind the Dentelles and sprayed white and pale yellow light in the morning mist. It reminded me of hard boiled eggs and champagne. And we stood with Monsieur Barruol by the door to his 'caves' and watched it silently until it was shining in our eyes.

Every day for the past week and a half, Monsieur le patron had been standing at the door of his caves. This was the first morning we had joined him.

"Now tell me again about this problem you are having," he said. He seemed to be only half-listening. He was still studying the sun.

"Beasts," I said again.

"Enormous beasts," Lorna said.

"They were running up and down across the ceiling last night. At first we were a bit frightened, if you want to know, but after that, we just lay there under the blankets and listened to them. But they were making too much noise for us to sleep."

"Terrible scuffling noises," Lorna said in English. "Tell him that they sounded like they were having a soccer match up there. Tell him that part." The idea of them all playing soccer above our heads had appealed to her in the middle of the night. But even with my head stuffed under a pillow, the thought of long-fanged beasts punting a ball back and forth in my attic didn't strike me as particularly intriguing.

"They were making terrible noises," I said.

"Did you see them?" He turned his head toward us, interested.

"No. They were in the attic."

"Ahhh! I think I know what they are. Did they make a noise like this?" He rattled his fingers across the rough wooden door.

"That's it!"

"Ahhh! The loirs!" He laughed. "It was the loirs! The dormice. But listen, those loirs aren't fierce beasts. They're very, very tiny. Like miniature squirrels. And they're very timides and gentils."

"These beasts aren't timides," I said. "They made a hell of a noise."

"No. They were the loirs. They always make a noise like that."

"How can we stop them?"

"You can't," he said. "But don't feel too badly. They won't make all that noise for very long. As soon as the nights get a little cooler, they will come out of your attic, and go outside, and dig a little hole in the ground." He made digging motions. "Then they will climb into the hole, and"—he folded his hands gently beside his head—"they will sleep."

"Ahhh," Lorna said.

"Of course if they are really bothering you, you can climb up into the attic and kill them all."

"Oh non non non! We wouldn't want to do that! We'll wait for it to get cooler."

"Good," he said. "It won't be long."

"Good."

Monsieur looked at his watch. "Eh bien. It's time I had another look at my wine."

"How's it coming?"

"Pretty well."

"Did you harvest a lot of grapes this year?"

"No. We were down about 25 per cent on what we usually get. But that's all right, because the quality is very good indeed. We were really lucky with the weather. Do you remember? The only close call we had was the afternoon that you and Madame came down to help."

"Yes, we remember."

"But other than that, it was perfect. I hear it was perfect all over the place. It should be an excellent year."

"Ah bon."

He turned and stepped through the door into his caves. "Come in if you wish, and I will show you around. It will help you to take your minds off the loirs."

"I have already forgotten them, Monsieur. Now that I know what they are and that they will soon leave, it doesn't matter,"

"And we were hoping for a tour," Lorna said. "That's one of the reasons we came down early when you wouldn't be so busy."

"Come then." He took us through the side door and into the first dark little room. The morning sun was lost. "These are my 'cuves'," he said. "They are great stone storage tanks dug into the floor, and they are very old." His voice echoed a bit in the enclosed space. "It is here that the grapes rest when they first come in off the vines." The air was thick with a dry musty smell like the one you notice when you first draw a cork on a bottle of dark red wine. "My cuves are very deep."

Monsieur stooped down beside a crude wooden trap door in the floor. "Listen." He cupped his hand around his ear over the old wooden boards. We all listened. "Hear it?" I heard nothing. "Come closer." I bent low over the door. Then, deep down in the cuve, I heard an unthinking, prehistoric rumble, very faint. And then higher up I could hear the little hissings and pinpricks of gas bubbling. "It's alive," he whispered. His eyes were shining. "It's working. Hear it? Hear it, Madame?"

"I hear it!"

Monsieur took us then to another part of his caves, where I had to duck under the spokes of the ancient white ceiling. He showed us his tiny laboratory. There, under a good fluorescent light were test tubes and instruments and complicated charts on the walls, and hourly notations. The laboratory seemed weirdly out of place in the Roman caves.

"I spend a lot of time in here these days," he said.

"We've noticed that. We've been seeing you at the door of your caves here every morning."

"It's important that I be here. Wine is a living material. You have seen that just now." He pointed back in the direction of the cuves. "From the moment that my harvest begins—and that as you know is an exact moment—until my wine is put in storage, it is living. It is like my children. When it is sick, I must attend to it and nurture it all hours of the day and night. When it is finally put down, it sleeps." He folded his hands beside his head sweetly, gently, like he did when he was telling us about the loirs.

Lorna and I tried to visualize the wine sleeping. I could still hear the faint prehistoric rumblings from the other room. "Come," he said. "I will show you some of the gas at work. But attention, eh? It can be very dangerous."

We tramped into a third room where there was a whole floorful of small trap doors. He edged down to the second door, back in the corner, and lifted the boards. "Don't get too close," he said. He fumbled in his pocket until he found his cigarette lighter. It was quite dark. I could see the white sparks flashing from the lighter as he spun the wheel. Then the orange flame. And when I looked down just a foot or two into the cuve, I could see the great purple mass of grapes lying there, stems and all. "Now watch," he said, as he lowered the flame towards the hole. Suddenly the fire went out. He pulled the lighter back, and lit it again. Then he lowered it again, and again it went out. He held the lighter down around the entrance to the tank and spun the wheel several times, making all sorts of white sparks, but no flame. "Gas," he said. "Poison gas. If you stuck your head in there for a few moments, you'd be truly dead." He slid the cover back over the cuve. "We won't touch these grapes now until after the gas has stopped."

Another day, a week or so later, Monsieur le Patron took me right down into that same cuve after the gas was gone. It was half empty by then, and he and his workmen had put a ladder down to shovel out the grapes. So I climbed down into the hole, and smelled the sweet warmth of the fermentation, and felt the intense dark heat that it had produced. All the residue was hot and purple, and the sweet damp walls of the cuve were warm.

Monsieur and his workmen shovelled out the residue, stuffed it into huge slatted buckets, and squeezed it in a powerful hydraulic press to take off the last of the juices.

They flowed hot and purple away from the press, out through a spout, and down a special hole in the floor. There was a lot of juice.

What was left over after the pressing was dry and purple and fibrous, and was thrown out the door. For weeks at that time of the year, wherever we went in that part of the Vaucluse, we would see the rough pressings, still shaped like the enormous slatted buckets that they had been pressed in, sitting beside the road waiting to be carried away. And everywhere we looked, the roads were stained purple.

But that first morning, Monsieur le patron had one more room to show us. It was dark, the floor was criss-crossed with pipes and the air was acrid with fumes. It tore at our eyes, clung and clawed in our throats and made us afraid to inhale. We would start to breathe in, and we'd feel the fumes pouring into our lungs like a dead weight, and we'd breathe out again, quickly, almost in a panic.

"Sulphur," said le patron, holding a cloth tightly over his mouth. "Smell it?"

"We can smell it."

We turned quickly back into the room with the many cuves sunk into the floor. "Sulphur is the only chemical I use," he panted. "None of this modern stuff to hurry along the fermentation or anything. No additives." He held a glass of cloudy purple liquid to the light and stared at it. "My wine is pure. It is made exactly the same way as the ancient Romans used to make it. Exactly." We stepped out into the sunlight, blinking. "It is like my children," he said again.

The sun was higher in the sky now. Monsieur Faucon, the postman, shot past in his yellow truck, making motions to let us know that there was mail in our box. There was shopping to do as well.

"We must go now, and leave you with your children," I said. "Thank you for the tour."

"Yes," said Lorna. "You have been very kind."

"Don't worry about those loirs," he said. "As soon as it is a little cooler, they will pack up and leave. Just as I have said."

17

Monsieur le Docteur Cherasse, head of obstetrics in the walled town of Carpentras, was the fastest writer I have ever seen. His expensive gold pen flew over the paper in sweeping horizontal motions, recording longhand our answers to his questions.

"Now. Do you have health insurance for this baby?" he asked us intensely.

"Not here. Only in Ontario."

"NothereonlyinOntario," he wrote. "I see," he said, tapping the gold pen on the pad. "Too bad. Too bad. The French government is very good about insurance you know. They pay all your drugstore bills, and all your hospital and doctor's bills. They even throw in a free layette for all prospective mothers. Too bad I can't get you on the French insurance."

"That *is* too bad."

Doctor Cherasse. Tough, young, competent. We had immediately liked him. He sat behind his desk studying us for a moment. His lean wiry body, his long pointed nose, and his ultra-high-strung temperament gave him an intense, bird-like quality. But his soft brown, intelligent eyes never let you believe for a moment that he could be cold.

"Bon, Madame," he said on our first visit to his office. "I must examine you. Follow me." He was up from his desk in a moment, and had swept her off into the adjoining examining room, leaving me alone in the little bureau to examine the wallpaper.

His office was very different from the first one we had visited in France. There were very few medical books. There was modern furniture, rough, green woven wallpaper, and pen-and-ink drawings of rare birds on the walls, with intense yellow beaks.

I remembered our first visit to a French doctor. It had been a kind of disaster. Lorna had been advised by Mary Henry, an American friend, not too long after we first arrived in Gigondas, to go in for a check-up. "I know you're being very clever and everything, having a baby over here," she had said. "But you're not a sturdy peasant girl who can drop a baby in the fields without missing a grape."

Mary had lived in France a long time. She had arranged an appointment for us with Doctor Blanc in the village of Bédoin, and we had arrived at the office at the designated time, armed with French dictionaries to help us wade through the medical terms, and clutching a sheaf of charts and records.

Doctor Blanc was a woman, and very young. Her office was large and imposing, overflowing with heavy antique furniture, paintings, bookshelves and stacks of grey medical journals. Because she was so young and attractive and full of humour, I figured that she needed a sombre room in order to make people believe that she really was a doctor, and not just a young girl playing a trick.

"Now." She had smiled across her heavy desk. "What seems to be the trouble?"

"Madame is pregnant," I said seriously.

"I can see that."

"We . . . we thought that she should come in so that you could have a look at her."

"Very good idea. Very wise. What's wrong with her?"

"Nothing," I had answered. Lorna wasn't able to speak much French at the time. I had to do the talking for her. "We just thought you should have a look."

"But I don't understand," she said. "If there is nothing wrong, why are you here?"

The logical simplicity of her question left me momentarily stunned. I scoured up and down my French vocabulary for a word for "check-up." Before I could answer, Madame le Docteur had turned to Lorna. "How many months have you, Madame?"

"Um . . . four."

"Four. Very good." She wrote that down. I felt relieved. We were making progress. "Do you get sick in the mornings?" she asked.

"No."

"Has the baby moved?"

"No."

"Have you put on any weight?"

"A little."

"Good! We will weigh you in that case." She took Lorna into her examining room, and gave her a careful lookover. "You're pregnant all right," was the only thing she said when she came back into her office. She wrote something down on a little piece of paper. "Here is the name of a good obstetrician who lives close by you. He is head of the maternity hospital in Carpentras. His name is Doctor Cherasse. You go and see him in a couple of months, or even in three months. There is no hurry. You are not in North America now." She smiled. "Unless you have a problem or want to ask some questions, stay home and enjoy your pregnancy. It can be a very satisfying time for you. If there is nothing wrong with you, why bother going to a doctor?"

We thanked her for her examination, and she stood up and politely shook hands with us over her desk. "How much do I owe you?" I asked.

"Nothing. I didn't do anything, so why should I charge?"

In the stream-lined examining room of Doctor Cherasse, I could hear him disconnecting the last of his highly sophisticated ultrasonic equipment. A moment later, he opened the door behind me into his office.

"Good," said Doctor Cherasse, as he darted back behind his desk. "Very good." Lorna came in and sat down beside me. "I'll write out a few instructions for the pharmacist. You can take the pills he will give you, and you won't have to come back here for a month." He picked up his pad and started to write.

We had already found out that in France, unless you are practically dying, the only place worth going to for medical advice is the pharmacy—never to a doctor. In Canada, it seemed as if unfortunate druggists had to go to school for twenty-five years so that they'd be allowed to empty the pills from a large wholesale bottle into a smaller retail bottle. Their pharmacists' degrees, plastered with green renewal stickers, are stuck up on a wall somewhere, collecting dust, while the druggists seem to be forced to abandon all their training in favour of scrupulous copying out of doctor's instructions.

But in France, being a pharmacist is a challenge. Everyone consults them. You can stand in front of the counter and recount your symptoms in hushed tones, while the druggist nods and clucks sympathetically, and after you are diagnosed, he will give you the proper pill. Or often, he won't recommend a pill at all. He might suggest instead that you get more rest, or take more exercise.

You can get weighed accurately in the pharmacy, or weigh a baby. And you can have various health check-ups done in the lab. A urinalysis, for example, can be done quickly and easily without the attention or expense of a doctor, and without the inevitable waiting in a dreary waiting-room.

Doctor Cherasse handed Lorna the prescription. "Madame," he said. "You have gained too much weight."

"What do you mean too much weight?" She was proud of her muscular dancer's figure. She still did her dancing exercises every day. "I haven't gained any weight."

"You'll have to go on a diet, Madame." His brown eyes sparked with instant decision.

"A diet?"

"Oui. Pas de pain," he said. He stroked the word off an invisible list in the air with his gold pen.

"No bread?"

"Et pas de fromage fermenté." He stroked it off the list.

"No fermented cheese?"

"Pas de sel."

"No salt?"

"Pas de porc."

"Ohhh."

"Pas de pasta."

"But I'm not fat!"

"You are, Madame. You are!" He said gleefully.

"Well . . . what about wine then? Can I drink wine?"

He looked up, surprised. "But of course, Madame. You can drink wine! It's good for you. But not too much," he scolded. "You could drink too much and . . . and perhaps fall down!"

18

When the season changed from summer to autumn, it didn't change over a period of time, melting gradually through a series of subtle nuances into another distinct time of the year. It fell on us fast, like someone spreading a cloak.

It changed the day we visited friends in a village just north of where we lived. Mary and Paul-Marc Henry were exciting people and very dear friends. Mary was an American: a striking, honey-blonde, who spoke perfect French with traces of a Virginia drawl. She was a writer of considerable talent, and a contributing editor for Vogue magazine in New York. Paul-Marc was French and fiercely beautiful, with a clutch of greying curly hair, snapping soft brown eyes, and arms like a wrestler's. He wielded his fierce intellect in many languages. When we were his neighbours, he was in charge of the Bangladesh Relief Programme for the United Nations. He stayed there throughout the war, and when he finally came home, he was as tired as any man I have ever seen.

We sat out all day at a marble table, and we basked in the hot sun, and ate fresh figs from the trees nearby. We drank a lot of fierce Grappa because it was good for the digestion, and tried some Cognac that wasn't so good. We sat under the olive trees with the pewter leaves and watched the olives turning black.

"These trees were reborn," said Paul-Marc. The sky was a harsh, clear blue as it always was. "They were killed off in the frost of 1956." The air was heavy like it always was with the smell of spices. "See that stump in the middle? That is the old stump. When the frost killed the trees, the roots just kept right on going, and grew again." From the table we could see for miles across the Plan de Dieu. "You can't kill olive trees. They're tough," he said. We drank some more Grappa. "Even a rough change of season won't stop them. They'll survive."

I listened to the very slight breeze clattering through their leaves. "They're a beautiful tree," I said.

"They're my tree," answered Paul-Marc. "The tree of my spirit."

Later on, the four of us went to see some property that our friends were thinking of buying in the country. We drove there in different cars, and we all saw the red light of the setting sun throwing pale reflections on the off-white walls of the big mas or farmhouses that we passed. Sometimes, we saw the crooked shadows of the pine trees as well.

At the property, we climbed the hill on foot, with the smell of thyme and rosemary hanging thick and close to the ground, with the voice of Paul-Marc echoing through the trees calling to his three dogs to stay close by, with the pine branches and scrub scratching our faces.

It was from the top of the hill that we discovered the change for the first time. When we looked down to the west, onto the Plan de Dieu, the prevailing colour was purple. Purple vineyards shouldering up to purple vineyards, with purple pines over to the east in a little valley. There was a faint purple haze rolling in on the Plan. Little orange farmhouses poked up here and there along the purple roads by the bridges. The air was smoky, and not clear.

When we had stood on the top of the hill for some time, admiring the view and surveying the property that could be bought, I turned around, looked up to the hill behind us and saw the moon through the pines. It was large and pale, almost white, and very bright indeed although it was still just twilight. The sky around the moon was a pale clear blue, not smoky like the air to the west.

When we drove home that night, we could see quite clearly in every direction. Everything was painted a medium blue that was so pure and uniform that it almost looked phoney. Like a flat in a theatre. The lights of Vaison and some of the other towns were the only variation on this colour.

The colours of Provence, the harsh, fierce, acrid, primary colours were immediately and completely gone. And in their place from that moment on were only smoky soft oranges, pastel yellows, and purples.

"They're like the colours of a faded painting from the Middle Ages," Lorna said. "Do you know what I mean? Those old colours were really true." She said this on the day we drove to Lafare and La Roque-Alric. We drove alongside slashes of pumpkin and ochre-coloured soil where it had been cut away to build the road. We saw how the uniformly green vineyards had all changed to colours that were very individual and sharply defined. They looked like a postage stamp collection if you were high enough up.

We passed a man riding home from work on a bicycle. He pedalled slowly and competently with a clip on his pant-leg, like a man who had been riding a bicycle all his life. Two chickens were tied over the handlebars.

And when it was night-time, when we had closed all the shutters and started a fire in the fireplace, we went for a walk down the Route des Florets towards the Chapelle de St. Cosme. We could smell the wood smoke from our fire, and hear our own footsteps on the hard pavement. It was cold and clear. All the softness and haze of the daytime had disappeared. It was a typical autumn night.

The full moon rose like a lamp through the mist above the Hotel des Florets and then settled coldly into the sky. It was clear all right. Clearer than we had ever seen it. We could see the individual tiles on the roof of the Chapelle de St. Cosme, and distinguish their separate shades of pink. We saw the dark leaves of the fruit trees where they had fallen onto the chalk-white soil of one of the upper vineyards. They looked like chocolates.

A jet flew overhead in the direction of Orly. It was up a good 30,000 feet. We could see the vapour trail very clearly. We could also see the jet.

"Let's take the car up the Route to the Saracen tower," I said.

"What for? Why don't we just go for a walk?"

"It's so clear. We could drive up there, and then take our walk high in the mountains. On a night like this, we could probably see right down into the Rhône valley."

"What makes it so clear here?"

"I don't know. Maybe there's no air pollution."

"Maybe it's the autumn."

It was cold. We rumbled all the way up the hill, wrestling past the parts of the road that were washed out, around the jagged, fallen rocks, past the tree that had tumbled into the road, through the 360 degree turn and up towards the Dentelles. We drove the whole way with our lights off. We could see almost as well as we could in the daytime. Every stone, every gully was clearly visible.

We stopped on a high part of the road by the Saracen tower. For a long time we didn't get out of the car. The silence was overpowering. But it was not a smothering silence like a cloak or a blanket. It was sharp and well defined. It was the sort of silence that you like to shatter, to break up, as you crack a field of new-fallen snow when you walk right through the centre of it.

I got out of the car, looked down over the side of the road, heaved a rock over the edge, and listened to it tumbling off down rock trails, scrabbling and cracking, making miniature landslides. It was a satisfying sound.

Lorna, who had lived much of her life in the mountains, said it was a dumb thing to do. "You can't throw rocks over the sides of mountains. You never know where they'll land. There could be somebody camping or something down there."

I listened to it still falling, and I didn't hear it hit anyone, but I didn't throw another.

Everywhere we looked, the landscape was lit up as if someone had snapped on a giant fluorescent street light, and although many of the colours that we could see weren't true to daylight colours, they were still distinguishable, tinged with pale blue.

Down below us was the Plan de Dieu, and the great vineyards of the Meffre family stretching off towards the horizon. We could see the endless rows of grapes, and I am sure if we had had a pair of binoculars, we could have seen the leaves on the vines.

Over in the direction of Orange, the headlights and tail-lights of the occasional car winked on and off as they passed between the plane trees and cabanots on the Plaine de Soleil.

The city of Orange seemed very close, and its lights shone orange and yellow with an occasional hint of red from the signs on the cafés downtown. Over to the south and a lot farther off, the lights of Avignon lay pale blue along the back of the Plaine like pearls. And above us was the Saracen tower, with every single ragged rock showing in the moonlight. Clear as a lightning bolt. It may have been our ears ringing, or it may have been some other subtle phenomenon that neither of us could explain, but when we stood quite still at the natural base of the crumbling fortress, we could hear a gentle, insistent electric hum in the air. We felt sure that mediaeval ghosts still lingered nearby.

"Something's changed," I told Lorna the next day. We drove through smoky shades of orange towards Vaison-la-Romaine. "Something's different."

"How do you mean?" We had been talking about writing books and about the weather.

"I don't know. Something's changed for me. It really has. But I can't lay my finger on just what it is. It's too soon to tell. Something has either begun, or finished. One or the other. But it's too soon to tell."

It wasn't until the next day, or even the day after that, that I knew what had finished. In the autumn, in our new home, with Lorna beside me with her belly swelling, I was purged. Somehow free. The resentment I had sensed towards anyone who had dared to call himself an artist in Canada, the stifling, dead feeling I had experienced in Toronto where I could not work, had left me. Perhaps being friends with the mayor, being saluted by the police chief, encouraged by the baker had something to do with the elation I was feeling. Perhaps it was the season. But I knew that the opinions of the people who didn't count would never affect me again. I knew that when I had to, I could go back to Canada, and never be bitter, or afraid, and never be bothered by the people that didn't count. All that was ended.

And if something hard to define had finished, something concrete had very surely begun. With the change of season, the soft yellow days, and the hard clear nights, I could feel the land and the influence of the soil tugging at me like gravity. Just like so many other artists in the Vaucluse before me or around me, I could feel my new book moving; and I began to work.

19

"Tiens. Tiens!" said Monsieur le curé. "That's curious. What's that sound?" He had come to talk about the mountain climbing. He put down his teacup.

"Just the loirs," we both answered.

"The what?"

"The loirs," I said. "The dormice. Don't you know about them?"

"No. Never heard of them," he said, looking up at the ceiling, listening.

"They're little beasts that live in our attic. They run around all night and make terrible noises," Lorna said. "We can hardly sleep some nights."

"Tiens!"

"They're not very big at all. They look like miniature squirrels. But they make as much noise in the attic as a pack of Labrador retrievers."

"Have you seen them?"

"Only once," I said. "I came downstairs one morning and found one in the living-room. At first I thought it was a giant mouse. But it ran round and round on the living-room floor, and then ran right up a wall."

"They have tiny hands," Lorna explained. "They can grip the little particles of plaster, and run right up a wall."

Monsieur le curé listened with his eyes closed, nodding his big white head absently. The subject hadn't quite captured his interest. "Do you know how it got into your living-room in the first place?" He was still thinking about climbing the mountain the next day.

"Yes," Lorna said. "They have a big hole in the wall over the stairs. They were running in and out of that hole all the time until Jamie blocked it up."

"It's bad enough that they make so much noise in the attic," I said. "I didn't want them running around in the living-room too."

"Good idea."

"Anyway, they should be quitting all this any night now. Monsieur Barruol told us that as soon as the season changed, they would go to sleep," she said.

"Curieux. Curieux."

"They're supposed to be asleep right now," I said. "But they refuse. They're the worst tenants imaginable."

"Interesting. Very interesting," he said, not really interested. He opened his eyes again and looked out of the window beside the table in surprise. "Oh! It's the night! C'est la nuit! I must go."

"But you must have some more tea! We must still discuss our climb tomorrow up St. Amand."

"Non non non non non. It's the night! I am afraid of the dark. I don't like to drive at night. I must be off." He jumped up from the table and pulled on his coat. "Besides, there's nothing more to discuss about the mountain. The weather will be good tomorrow. Just come and meet me in my churchyard at about 1:30, and I'll have everything arranged." He shook hands with us both. "And don't worry, Madame. Even in your condition, it won't be a difficult climb."

Even early the next morning, we could tell it was going to be a good day. For several days it had been cloudy and overcast, and the temperature hadn't been high enough first thing in the morning for us to go out without our coats.

But Monsieur was quite a capable amateur weatherman—like most of the Provençaux. At 8:00 a.m. it was already warm, and to the east the sky over the Dentelles was already clear and blue. By 9:00 a.m., when I stepped out to pin back the shutters and let in the light, the lizards were playing on the plaster walls, soaking up the sun. We hadn't seen them for days. They scuttled in under the shutters when they saw me coming, moving so fast that it was hard for the eye to follow them. And when I swung the shutters on their creaking hinges, they would be off again to a new hiding place, fast as a handclap.

Monsieur le curé looked truly splendid standing out in front of his church. The tiny Vacqueyras courtyard was filled with sunlight. He was wearing a new navy sweater, which was the only different piece of clothing in which we ever saw him and it made him look robust and powerful. A couple of pigeons clattered up from the curry-coloured belfry, and floated down into the courtyard just ahead of the car. His cheeks were rosy, and his white hair bristled out from under his dark blue beret. We had never seen him wearing a beret before. I stopped the car in the sunlight without disturbing the pigeons. He had a leather binocular case over his shoulder. He looked like a guerilla from the Spanish Civil War.

"You have come!" he boomed. "I thought you might have forgotten!" His rich voice filled the courtyard.

"Of course we hadn't forgotten. How could we? It will be such an adventure climbing this mountain, eh?"

"Mais oui!" We shook hands all round. He was full of life. "The weather is perfect. Impeccable!" He bounded into the Volkswagen, filling the seat, and slammed the door so hard I was afraid it would disintegrate in his hands.

"We should stop on the way to St. Amand, if it isn't too much trouble," he said. "I want to see how my olives are doing."

"Your olives?"

"But of course. I have some special trees where they grow wild by one of the old mineral water sources. It's getting to be nearly time to pick them. They are up in the hills. You will see." We drove away from the village of Vacqueyras. "And the little beasts in your attic. They did not disturb you, I hope. You slept well?"

"Yes. Last night they weren't so bad. Perhaps they will leave us soon."

We rumbled up the hills on the far side of Beaumes-de-Venise, past the gypsum mine, up to a level place where the lime trees were growing and the soil was about the colour of dried mustard. "Stop the car! This is it. My olives!"

I pulled the car off the road as well as I could, and Monsieur was up and out of his seat and banging the door before I could even shut off the engine. "Come!" he shouted. He disappeared up an invisible trail through a clump of pomegranates. We followed. The ground was covered with rosemary. Good, strong, fresh rosemary. We gathered it in clumps for cooking with lamb.

There were some places where the spices grew better or were more powerful. The thyme in the remote alpine valleys on the west side of Mont Ventoux, for example, seemed especially heady. This rosemary was particularly good. I could tell. Spices were another thing we were learning about. Store-bought spices, even locally grown store-bought spices, had begun to taste inferior to us. Mouldy and old, and almost inedible. "Come!" he boomed. "Vite!"

His little olives were growing in a ravine just at the edge of the source. "The sulphurous water makes them especially good, I think. Anyway, they look very good this year. There will be a great many. In about a month, they'll be touched by the first frost and ready to harvest." I tasted one that had already turned black. It was so bitter it nearly lifted the back off my mouth.

"You can come and get some here if you wish," he said. "Now that you know where they are."

"Thank you." I coughed unthankfully.

We were able to stop the car part way up St. Amand. We didn't have to walk the whole way. And when we did have to walk, there were signs to follow, and a trail, and red marks splashed on the rocks. Monsieur led the way, his cheeks red in the sunlight, his eyes smiling, using a walking stick he had found by the edge of the trail. "Tiens. I see that my marks have lasted well," he said. "But some of the signs are missing."

"Oh?"

"Vandals."

"Too bad!" we said, climbing, picking our way through the rocks.

"No. Not so bad as some years. Most of the signs are still here. I make this climb once a year, you see. Just for the fun of it."

We crossed through a place open to the sunlight where a landslide had ripped through the forest. Great jagged rocks lay everywhere, and a savage slash extended right up to the top of the mountain.

We worked our way around to the north slope, where the going was far more vertical. We padded through a lush forest in the shade where the tree trunks arched tall and gothic. The path was steep and slippery with leaves and hard to climb. "Doucement!" Monsieur would call out, his voice echoing a bit in the narrow enclosed space, as in a cathedral. "Take it easy, Madame. We have plenty of time. You must be careful of your baby." I could see tiny puffs of white breath as he spoke. It was cold in the shade.

Finally we came out above the trees, and worked our way up a natural staircase, and through some empty countryside that looked like a Greek shepherd's landscape. Not long after that we eased precariously over the lip and up to the top.

We sat down to rest at the base of an old cross, erected in memory of someone whose name was lost. The cold and the wind had chattered away most of the letters. We sat on the leeward side of the cross and studied the landscape through Monsieur's binoculars. There was a constant wind.

We could see all the villages through 270 degrees. The Dentelles were southwest of us, and shrouded in haze. They looked like silver sails, especially through the binoculars.

The top of St. Amand was basically flat, and the ground was covered with a strong hardy thyme. We gathered some of that. One edge of the table was riddled with wonderful old caves, and we had to watch our footing, because there were hidden holes in the grey underbrush, and dark drops. Walls and foundations of an ancient, probably prehistoric village were scattered near the caves, all overgrown with stunted brush. We wondered what band of troglodytes would have lived so far up, and in such an isolated and inhospitable place.

It was an hour before we decided that we had seen enough. On our way down we took it easy and nobody slipped. Monsieur le curé and I helped Lorna over the tougher spots, both of us feeling very gallant. I was proud of her.

Her doctor on the other hand wasn't nearly as impressed with her physical prowess as we were. When he heard the story, he stripped us of all our bravery and gallantry with a single flick of his gold pen. But it had been an easy climb, and Lorna told me that it hadn't been at all hard for her, although we were both tired when we got back to the car. Monsieur le curé wasn't tired at all.

Suzette is a very old and isolated village in the mountains. It crouches grey on a hilltop, as if it were carved out of a single piece of stone. When we got to the main intersection of the town on our way home, the road was blocked and crowded with men, all standing and shuffling back and forth, talking about the weather and the crops.

Monsieur le curé had already forgotten that he had just climbed a minor mountain. He urged us to stop right in the centre of the road when he saw the crowd, and banged out the door in mid-sentence with the car still rolling. We were too tired to follow him. We watched him dash red-faced into the centre of a knot of acquaintances, pumping hands.

Monsieur was a conservationist. On the top of the mountain we had found a high, fenced enclosure, shut off like a fortress. "Keep Out!" the signs around the enclosure read. "Experimental area set up for studies of Conservation! ECOLOGICAL AREA!" All around the base of the fence were empty wine bottles, old sardine cans, and bits of board left over from the fence's construction. Le curé had angrily gathered up all the refuse, muttering dire, untranslatable things as he did this. And then, with a monumental toss, he heaved everything over the fence onto the ecological side. "Idiots," he declared, shaking a fist at the criss-crossed wires. "Here's to your kind of conservation!"

All the men standing on the road talking to Monsieur had one eye on the one-room schoolhouse on the corner. They were waiting for their children to come out from their classes. The farmers among them were shuffling in their muddy boots and rough work shirts, talking about the price of olives. Some of the farmers, strong, ruddy and healthy, smelling of fresh straw and vin ordinaire, were only my age. They faced the setting sun, smiling and keeping one eye on the door of the school. They looked tough and unafraid and at peace. Maybe it was the setting sun.

Then the door of the school flew open, and the grey asphalt courtyard filled with children in their brightly coloured, good school clothes, calling and shouting, running to their fathers standing in the road looking very proud. The teacher came out last and locked the door. He was wearing a white English sweater and had long dark hair. He talked to two of the children in the courtyard, waved to a father whom he knew in the road, and lit a cigarette.

Monsieur le curé patted a couple of excited heads, and said a few soft words to another little one who was shy, and then dived back into the car, popping our eardrums with the air pressure as he slammed the door.

"We can take a short cut home over a private road if you wish," he said. "Monsieur Bonfils there has just given us permission."

"Fine."

"Of course, it's not really a short cut . . . but it is more beautiful than the other road."

"You're not too tired, Monsieur?"

"Of course not! The day is young! But . . . perhaps Madame is too tired."

"I'm not tired. Just so long as we don't have to get out of the car."

"We won't. Drive on! There's a little road. You will see."

The narrow road just south of Suzette wound up through the pines and the fig trees to a point where we could see far out into the valley.

Just down the road from us, one of the farmers was cultivating the soil around his olive trees. It was far too small and precarious a field for a tractor. He had a single-bladed plough hitched behind his horse. The going was rough. The horse had to make tight turns, back up, and duck its head under the lower branches of the olive trees. We could hear the man shouting to the horse, urging it on in a series of friendly tones. "It's Monsieur Marchand," said the priest. "I'll just step out for a moment and say hello to him."

With the engine off, we could hear the Provençal orders to the horse echoing musically up and down the valley. Monsieur Marchand had been alone with his horse and his olives until we came along. We could tell they were friends.

The soil was blood red. We could see that, even in the haze, and even though the sun had already set.

20

If you go to Carpentras after 10:00 a.m. on market day, you might as well not go at all. The egg ladies will have nothing to sell. The fish man will shrug his shoulders over his empty stall, and the streets will be packed and churning with people, fighting for the last of the leftovers with fistfuls of francs.

Let there be no mistaking it. The French are serious about eating and about shopping. What other nation, with an average family income approaching that in Canada, would spend 40 per cent of the pay cheque every week on food?

If we got up at the proper time, and struggled out the door, it would be cool and clear above the house, with the sun not yet out from behind the mountains. Often, on the road between Gigondas and Carpentras we would catch a glimpse of Mont Ventoux which was by far the highest peak in the area, austere and snow-covered, already bright in the sunlight, with the five-storey television station on the summit looking more like a thin white pole than a building. Then ahead of us in a valley, we would see the top of the ancient Cathédrale St. Siffrein in Carpentras, poking up through the mist, while the rest of the town was completely obscured. If it weren't for the top of the Cathédrale, you might think that Carpentras was a lake.

It would be too early for the sun to have touched the twisted streets of the old ville. If we saw that morning mist, we would know that we had beaten the crowd.

We liked to leave the car in the Allée des Platanes where there was always a parking space, and head up the narrow side streets that the sun hadn't yet touched, towards the centre of town. We would walk past the crumbling church with Latin inscriptions over the door, sadly transformed into a very dirty repair shop; past some sleeping dogs, and down past some of the most beautiful doors in Carpentras. Haunting stone figures were carved above some of them, some had brass fittings and lilting Provençal patterns, some were completely restored, and some were off their hinges. A clump of Algerians would bustle up the narrow street, their voices bouncing damply off the walls, their dark brown eyes shining proudly out from under their brown woollen helmets. They didn't like the cold. Several French housewives would dart past us, chattering away at high speed, clutching empty shopping baskets as they disappeared around a corner into the mist.

If we were very lucky, if we timed it just right, we would arrive at the foot of the Cathédrale and the open Place, just in time to catch the first real passes of the sun.

The Carpentras market is enormous. It stretches in all colours all the way across town from the ancient gates of the Port d'Orange, to the Place de l'Hôpital. The last hangers-on in the market spill down the steps across the road from the Hôtel-Dieu in a sort of clinging limbo—half in the market, half out. The whole market must cover an area of the downtown of more than a square mile.

The market people parade like gypsies from one town to another. Each one has his allotted space in each town, and the established merchants get to know you after a while, so that if there were some dissatisfaction with a purchase one week, you could always come back the next week and burn the ear off the appropriate man. They all straggle in with the pale light of dawn, some of them nose to tail like caravaners, each mushrooming up his display in the early morning. By the time the crowds begin to arrive, the merchants have created an illusion of permanence out of wobbly tents and unwieldy trailers and filled the market with shouts of colour and sound, until you would think it was there forever.

But just as the second hand crosses twelve, when all the south grinds to a halt for the traditional three-hour lunch, the market closes down like someone slamming a door. And then the streets are empty. It is done for another week.

"Buy my spices! Véritable spices of Provence!" shouts the spice lady in the sun just past the Cathédrale. "Anis vert-basilic-laurier-romarin-sauge-et-thym!" she shouts, making it all one word. Her hair grows stiff and straight out of her head like scratchy grey clumps of thyme. "These are the best spices in the market! Don't go to anyone else!" Her makeshift table in front of the Prisunic is crowded with plastic sacks of dull green spices, all home picked. Some of the spices are stacked beside the table on the ground.

We stride down the street, past the edge of the dry goods section, where cloth is being sold in great coloured bolts, and a Mediterranean street hawker has drawn a crowd. "THIS is what I'm going to do!" he shouts, his voice echoing, beads of sweat standing on his dark forehead, his small crooked body bent forward, straining at the customers, pulling at them. "I'm not going to sell this beautiful blanket for it's usual price—I'll cut the price in *half!*" He throws the blanket into the air so that it opens. He twirls it, it catches the sun. "And then I'm going to cut off yet another franc! And another! And right now I'm going to offer it for the lowest price in all of France! BOUM!" He smacks the top of the blanket suddenly. "Just like THAT!" Not even one of his French audience stirs, or flickers an interested eyelid. They are watching the free show. Not buying blankets.

We push on down the street, past the place where the heepies sell their handicrafts. They have a small table, filled with belts and odds and ends of leather and some homemade jewellery. Everything is extremely crudely made, and is sold at hopelessly high prices. We never see them sell anything, but they are there every week.

There is another rough stand nearby, and an Algerian wearing heavy sunglasses sells religious literature. "Jésus sauve!" the signs shout. "Come here to be saved! Now is the time!" And then there are all sorts of squiggly Arabic letters that we can't read. He isn't selling anything either.

At the corner is the old man with the donkey. The donkey is rheumatic and docile and has grey fur that smells like dust. Little saddle bags are slung over his furry back filled with things to sell. The donkey is a sales gimmick.

We march around the corner, ignoring the donkey completely, and cross over to the fish market—the best fish market that we know of. Great wide tables are set up under the damp arcades, lined with an incredible variety of seafood. The man who looks after us, and who knows us, looks like a Dutch fisherman with his navy blue cap with a black vinyl peak. He wears a red sweater, a full-length yellow plastic apron tied around his neck, and clumping rubber boots.

A whole fresh tuna straddles the end of his table, with a head as big as a man's. We watch le patron carve off great fresh tuna steaks, cutting crosswise through the back of the fish—dark red cross-cut sections, two inches thick—with his broad sharp knife. The blade moving through the heavy red mountain of meat like a razor.

There are rays, mackerel, herring, fresh sardines, whitefish, sole, cod, and conger eels and very deep water fish that we can't identify. They lie there translucent with no colour and enormous frog-like eyes.

"Two fine trout, if you please, and some fresh moules."

He reaches two slick rainbow trout like torpedoes out of his basket and tosses them onto the scales. They are cheaper than most meat. "You'll have to get the moules from my son," he says in his thick Marseilles accent.

"Okay."

We struggle through the crowd over to the shellfish section, with our two trout in a plastic bag. "A kilogram of mussels, please."

"What kind?" asks his son.

"Do you have any Spanish ones?"

"No. They're all sold out." One of the live crabs gets up out of its bin, spindles stealthily over to the Coquilles St. Jacques, and nestles down among them, spitting foam.

"Give me a kilo of moules from the north then."

"Oui, Monsieur." He snatches up the pale brown crab, and tosses it back into its proper bin. One of the Coquilles snaps shut its shell. He scoops up the black mussels, cold and alive, out of a dark wicker basket, weighs them, picks us a nice bunch of parsley, and tosses in a bright yellow lemon. "My compliments," he says. "Good appetite."

Our next stop is the olive man on the corner. He sells everything in bins. Seeds, dried beans, rough yellow corn flour, dates, and at least four different kinds of olives. We buy olives of the region: black, dark, salty, and absolutely necessary for the hors d'oeuvres and Provençal cooking. If all I had to eat were harsh black olives, pasta with cheese, and a glass of throaty vin ordinaire, I would be happy.

He scoops up his olives with a small wooden shovel, and weighs them for us on his scale. He is a little wiry man with dark olive skin, and black eyes that smile out at us from under his peaked cap. "These olives are very cheap this week," he says.

"I know," I answer. "And they are certainly the best in the whole market." I eat another one from his bin.

"Thank you, Monsieur. You are very kind."

The saffron man looms over his grim little stand in the corner at the end of the arcade. Saffron is practically the only thing he sells. He shifts from one foot to the other looking like an elegant gentleman recently torn from the aristocracy, painted with a one-day growth of beard and tossed into the market. It is cold and damp at his end of the arcade. He speaks with a softly cultured accent. The saffron for the mussels costs nearly as much as the mussels.

We turn around after leaving the saffron man and retrace our steps on the opposite side of the street. We walk past a mobile butcher shop, with sausages and smoked hams hanging, and past a stand filled with cheap plates and knicknacks. On the ground beside them is the simplest type of stand of all: two Africans hover over a purple cloth they have spread on a patch of empty pavement, displaying two or three pieces of questionable African jewellery.

But we push past them all, and into a store close by where we like to buy our beer—at 10¢ a bottle. Two quart bottles. One for the moules. One for the trout. The smiling lady there adds up our purchases with a stub of a pencil on a torn corner of yellow paper.

We buy a pot of Provençal honey—strong and harsh and golden, like our area. It comes from the slopes around Mont Ventoux, where bees can collect pollen from endless acres of wild lavender. Some milk—100-day milk that you can store on a shelf. "And some coffee, please."

"Oui Monsieurdame," she says, adding it all up on the torn bit of paper.

Next door is the cheese store, where they sell a good number of the 300 King Cheeses of France. The store is brightly lit and cheery, and the heavy smell of 300 varieties of cheese struggles out the door.

"Yes Monsieurdame?" the lady asks.

"Una livra de beurra, please," Lorna says, pronouncing it all proudly with a Provençal accent.

"Haute qualité?"

"Oui."

She tosses her thin steel wire over the yellow mountain of butter, and then, holding the two ends firmly, draws the wire in towards her, and in one silent stroke lobs off an enormous chunk that always looks too big, but is usually within a gram or two of being right on. She has a good eye.

"And a nice Bleu de Bresse," I say. "But not too ripe. I like them a little unripe."

"Oui, monsieur." Her hand darts into the pile of cheeses and she pulls out just the right one. She takes off the cardboard lid, and lets me smell the cheese, and poke it appreciatively.

Orange Goudas shoulder up to a great lacy piece of Gruyère. There is a Roquefort in its foil wrapping that they cut with a knife into pieces like a crumbling blue cake. Up high on a shelf are brightly coloured rows of jam in chubby glass pots with paper lids. Made in the maison, and almost as expensive as eating Roquefort.

"Will there be anything else, Monsieurdame?"

"I don't think so," I said, sadly feeling the bottoms of my pockets. "We have several places to go yet, Madame."

"Thank you, Madame," Lorna adds.

"I am at your service."

The delicious smell of pizza hangs in the air. We know where it's coming from. There is a crowded red and white pizza stand just down the street where they cook the pies in portable gas ovens. We never buy any though, because it never looks as good up close as it smells. Up close there is only the odd black olive or anchovy scattered pathetically in a desert of tomato and cheese. Nobody can make pizza except Americans.

At the egg stand, the ladies sell nothing but farm-fresh eggs. They are even graded in different sizes, just as they are in Canada, but they are all brown eggs and very cheap. We buy two, three, even six in a paper sack, and listen to the tired tune the man plays on his accordion across the street.

He is always there. Always in the same place. It is his stand. We pay for the eggs and tramp over to the vegetable stand on the opposite corner. He crouches on a battered three-legged stool, playing the same pathetic ditty, over and over each week. Tapping his tired foot, looking at nobody, sometimes smoking a cigarette as he plays. We buy some cabbage and some artichokes and some very nice spinach. Two ancient dogs sprawl at the man's feet. They are both dressed up in party costumes—

tiny hats and frilly collars and eyeglasses balancing on their noses. They always look the same. They never do anything. Their trick is just to squat there shaking by the money bowl, wearing the clothes. They don't jump through hoops or anything. The lady in the vegetable stand wants to cut us a mammoth chunk of orange squash, but we have plenty to eat already. Some apples though. We need some golden apples.

Those poor dogs. They are so old. It's all they can do to lie at his feet by the money bowl and not tremble so much that their glasses slide off their white whiskered noses.

We pay the vegetable woman, and push north towards our last two stands. The achromatic little man with the accordion hunches his shoulders and swings into another identical chorus with his foot tapping.

We know one stand at the north end where they sell very good dates on the branch. The young couple in charge always likes us to sample them, and some of their other dried fruit as well. The branches of dates are sometimes tied in bunches and hung up for display. We buy some dried figs and dried prunes, and taste some dried apricots. They have a bin of walnuts, and a display of dried bananas. One time we bought a powerful rope of garlic from them. Each bulb was tinged purple and firm. We hung the rope in the kitchen when we got home, and used it all winter.

The little flower lady isn't old. She sits alone behind her table and under her tarpaulin. Her fingernails are dirty from working in her garden, and she wears a flowered smock. We buy a couple of francs' worth of multi-coloured anemones, and she helps us pick out a good bunch. She pushes her dark hair back over her ears with one hand as she hunts for change for us in her tin box.

In the next stall, a man is selling sheep's heads—all skinned and scrubbed with dark blue eyes. But we don't buy anything, because we have finished shopping and are tired, and I can't think what I would do with a sheep's head.

So we leave. The market is still filling up with people and becoming increasingly frantic. We pass under the dark Port d'Orange that was built in the fourteenth century. Two fish stands compete against each other under the arch. You have to watch your step because the ground is slippery with fish heads, and a live green crab or two is trying to sneak off across the pavement to some hiding place. There is a scrawny cat nearby, and a desperately old dog with white whiskers and one smoky, bad eye. His fur hangs on him like a worn-out bear rug tossed over a piece of furniture in an attic to keep off the dust. The two animals are waiting side by side for a good moment to steal into the dark archway for a seafood snack.

It is cold under there. The sun hasn't warmed it yet, and one of the women fish vendors jams her cold red hands into her apron pockets and yells out the names of the fish she has to sell in a long, broad, echoing monotone. All in Provençal.

21

"Jamie," she said in the early morning, "I think there's someone coming to the door."

"It can't be. No one would dream of coming here this early. You're hearing things."

It had been one of those grey, cool, late autumn mornings when neither of us had wanted to get up. We had poked around puffy-eyed in the kitchen without saying much to each other except in low mutters. Neither of us was dressed, and we had only opened the shutters on the front door. The rest of the house was black.

"I tell you, I can hear footsteps," she insisted. She darted off into the bathroom, pulling at her robe, and leaving me to struggle to the door in my underwear. At that moment, someone began tapping loudly, urgently on the glass outside, with a key or other metal object.

When I got to the door, I discovered the great black shape of Monsieur le curé on the other side of the glass, staring in, shading his eyes with a smooth pink hand. When he saw me coming he stepped back slightly from the glass, and with his florid face beaming, he made a gesture of surprise and delight.

"I thought you'd gone out shopping," he boomed in the hallway. "All your shutters were closed, and it is so dark in here, that I thought you'd gone." His voice echoed happily through our tiny house. He was so excited he didn't notice I was only dressed in my underwear.

Lorna appeared then, smiling shyly in the doorway of the bathroom, wearing her robe, the most noticeable tangles swept out of her hair. Le curé reached up in delight when he saw her, and tore off the little round Turkish hat he was wearing, exposing his great white head. "Ah! Bonjour Madame! I thought you had both gone. And I have such good news!"

"Good news?"

"Oui! I have solved it!" he shouted happily. "I have the solution to your problem. I have been busy at home all morning in my study doing research, and when I found the answer to your problem, I came right over."

"Problem?"

"Oui. The beasts, my children. The beasts." He started to yank off his crumbling black coat. Lorna helped him. I was still dazed by his sudden exuberant arrival. "Why they're not beasts at all," he said. "They're loirs!"

"We know that. We told you that."

"But they are fine beasts. They are so sympathiques, so timides. They are very gentils. A fine addition to any household."

"You can have them."

"Oh, but they are so beautiful. I have seen pictures of them."

"They may be beautiful to look at," I said. "But they're not so beautiful to listen to. They won't let us sleep."

"Ah! But they will sleep! They should be asleep already. I found this out this morning. When the fall comes, they are supposed to go out. They dig a little hole in the ground, they fill their stomachs with food, and . . . they sleep." He folded his hands under his head, just as Mr. Barruol had.

"I don't know. It's getting pretty late in the season. And they're showing no signs of sleeping at all."

"But there is a famous expression in France, 'Dormir comme un loir,' to sleep like a loir. They say that about a person who sleeps too much or is habitually lazy."

"Our loirs don't sleep too much," I said. "In fact, I don't think they sleep at all."

Lorna steered the priest towards a living-room chair. "Please sit down, Monsieur," she said. "We're just making some coffee."

"Non non non. I can't sit! I can't sit! I'm in a hurry. But I want to see your loirs. There must be something wrong with them that they won't sleep. It is time." He dashed around the living-room table squinting up at the ceiling. "There must be a trapdoor somewhere to look up into your attic."

"Mais oui, Monsieur. It's in the bathroom."

"Ahhhh!" He immediately sprinted off into the bathroom. "C'est ça. C'est ça! Quick! Do you have a ladder?"

"But you're not going to look up there?"

"But of course. Why not? There must be something wrong with them that they won't sleep."

"But they might fly at you!"

"Jamie's afraid to look up there," Lorna added helpfully.

"Nonsense. They are so timides. So gentils. Quick! The ladder!"

We found the ladder, and he had us both hold the base steady while he climbed unhesitatingly, almost at a dead run. He threw open the trapdoor in the ceiling, and disappeared into the hole until only his legs were showing, wobbling a bit on the shaky old steps. "Tiens. Tiens." His voice sounding hollow and far off. "Tiens, tiens. Curieux."

"What? What is it?"

He started back down the ladder. "Nothing there," he said. "There is no one in your attic."

"We have another attic," Lorna volunteered.

"Where?"

"Upstairs. Just on the landing at the top of the stairs."

"Allez!" he shouted, snatching and folding the ladder in one deft motion, and running for the stairs.

We held the base again as he climbed. This time I was very worried that he might fall. Because if he did, he would probably tumble right down the stairs. "Tiens. Tiens," he said again, wobbling precariously, his voice muffled. "They must be hidden somewhere. I can't see them." He bounded down the ladder.

We all tramped back down the stairs together. The priest was shaking his head solemnly, a bit perturbed that he hadn't solved the problem after all. I was carrying the ladder.

Suddenly, halfway down the stairs, he stopped dead. "Mais, qu'est-ce que c'est?" he asked, pointing to a small hole in the wall.

"That's the hole we were telling you about."

"That's how the loirs were getting into our living-room," I said.

"Jamie blocked it up, remember? He didn't want them in the house as well as in the attic."

"Just a minute," he boomed happily. "I think I have it." He sprinted down the stairs, and over to the huge Provençal fireplace in the corner of the living-room. Without hesitation, he leapt right up onto the hearth, ducked under the mantel, and disappeared up the chimney except for his feet. "Oui oui oui oui oui. I have it!" He emerged from the fireplace like a great sooty Santa Claus. We watched in amazement as he came back up the stairs, and yanked the stopper out of the hole.

"But I don't understand. Now the loirs will be able to run around the living-room again," I said.

"You must let them. They won't hurt anything. They just come down into the living-room to go out the chimney. Don't you see? They climb up the chimney, they go out, they dig a little hole in the ground, and . . . they sleep. It is simple!"

Lorna and I looked at each other incredulously. "You mean, they were making all those restless noises at night because they wanted *out?*"

"Of course! They were restless because you wouldn't let them sleep. They must fill their bellies, you see, before they sleep."

"No wonder they used to make concerted efforts to push out that stopper," Lorna said. "They were starving up there!"

"But of course!" he said. "And that one you saw in your living-room, Monsieur, he was just late coming back to his nest. You just happened to catch him en route from the chimney to his hole."

"Why of course!"

"And now," he said, "you must put some grapes and apples and things in your fireplace to lure them out. They are very frightened by this experience. Tonight, they will smell the food, come down, fill their bellies and . . . out the chimney!"

"Monsieur," I said. "You are a genius. A true scientist."

"Come and have some coffee now," Lorna said.

"Non non. My heart, you know." He thumped a pink finger on his black barrel chest. "And besides, I'm in a hurry." He sped to the door, crushing his little round Turkish hat onto his head as he went. "You know? Someone should do a scientific study on you Canadians." He pulled on his overcoat. "You must be impervious to the cold."

"How do you mean?"

"How else could you stand it like that? Running around in your underwear!" He slammed the door behind him, and was gone.

22

"Oh, ça change," old Madame Galon in the bakery said. She had to bend far over from the waist in her black dress so that she could see the patch of sky through her window. "The weather changes."

The Mistral wind had come that morning very early and without warning. It tore at the tiles of the roof, it broke a window in our garden cabin, it hunted around all the corners of our house searching out dark hiding places, and filled our house with smoke from the fire. It roared down from the north, and scoured the plains along the Rhône clean of the haze and soft light. It left in its place a pure grey light, clear as crystal, that was like facing a moment of truth.

"Et ça pousse, eh?" she said, pointing to Lorna's belly. "Ça pousse. It sprouts well."

"Oui, Madame, like the weather, it changes, it sprouts. There are just two and a half more months."

Hidden around the bends on the winding route on the other side of Sablet, down past the ancient walled town of Séguret, were thin sheets of verglas, spread across the road like traps. The verglas, which is a black ice, seeps up through the pavement and is almost invisible—and impossible to drive on. "Route Dangereuse 3 Km.," said the yellow sign on the way to Vaison-la-Romaine. "Verglas!"

We could see Mont Ventoux when we drove in, and some of the peaks of the Hautes-Alpes. They were covered in white snow, looking sharp and sober in the air, as if encapsulated in some static atmosphere where time had stopped. You could look at them the same way you would look into the side of a goldfish bowl, or at a picture.

All along the Grand Rue in Vaison-la-Romaine colourful posters were displayed in the shop windows, telling about the art shows in the tiny mountain villages of the area. One poster advertised a permanent photography exhibition in a village just a kilometer or two away. Another town was publicizing its annual pottery show. The village of Séguret, with a population of 672, advertised its exhibition of the works of 400 artists, from twenty-eight countries and four continents.

Crowded in the windows of the shops off the Place de Monfort were the little hand-carved or molded clay figures called santons. There are over seventy of these figures in various standard sizes depicting all the traditional residents of a Provençal village—the mayor, the woodcutter, the spinner, the shepherd. Every family collects the tiny figures in a size they can afford for their Christmas crèche. Through an ancient stretching of artistic licence, and an even more delightful leap in time, these seventy-two figures crowd into the typical Provençal family crèche and shoulder right up to the more traditional three kings and babe in the manager.

We shopped for groceries in the small stores off the Place, and studied the innumerable fancy pastries and homemade chocolates that you can find in such abundance in Vaison. Chubby pots of homemade jam lined the windows, with their lids wrapped in squares of red and white checkered cloth.

Down the street, at the butcher shop on the Grand Rue, a wild boar was hanging out in front of the window on two great iron hooks. Dark, fierce, and enormous. His famous tusks had been sheared off, but his body was shaped like a powerful bullet. I touched his bristly hide in wonder. Local people stepped around the boar almost unnoticing, putting one foot down off the sidewalk onto the road to get by.

When Carolyn Caughey, a knowledgeable friend of ours, visited us from Canada, she saw the same wild boar hanging there and nearly fell out of the car in surprise. "I can't believe it!" she said. "It's incredible. I always thought that wild boars were mythical creatures—like unicorns or centaurs or something." We told her that they still run wild in the Dentelles, even though this area has been permanently settled for 2,000 years. The year before we came, Monsieur Barruol saw one snuffling mythically right through our front yard.

We left Vaison by the Old Bridge, which has been in constant use for those 2,000 years, and took the slow route home through the villages on the other side of the Ouvèze River. At

Rasteau, we stopped in the main Place to get some vegetables at a little store we knew there. The entire town was dead silent. It was just a minute or two before noon. The sky was still grey, and it was quite cool, but the Mistral wind had disappeared.

When we came back out of the store into the Place, there was a clattering in the rusty dry leaves of the plane trees overhead. It was beginning to snow. We stopped and listened to the sound the snow made. There was no other sound in the whole village. The crunchy kernels squeaked under our feet as we crossed to the car. In the centre of the Place was a statue, already powdered white, and under it was written:

For the Children of Rasteau
1914-1918
Dead for la France.

Outside Courthézon that day, we discovered the Château Causans. It is entirely walled in, like a fortress from the road, with many of the outbuildings and homes of the workers built right into the wall, but facing inwards for protection. At one end, the gates were open, and we could see down through the barnyards, through the full lofts and the straw bales, some of which had spilled out into the courtyard and collected roofs of snow; past an ancient blue ox cart, past a dog standing in the narrow lane, puffing clouds of white breath, with tiny flecks of snow clinging to his hot dark back; to the four red-roofed towers of a real, working château.

In the snow, everything was peaceful and silent. Like Mont Ventoux, the Château looked like a picture, or something from the seventeenth century encapsulated under glass.

Just as Madame Galon had told us, the season had changed to winter. The air became clear again and the skies were either cloudless, or else heavily overcast. When it became cooler still at night, when we banked up the fire carefully before going to bed, it would have been easy to believe that it would snow right through until January. Some years it may happen like that. But we didn't see snow again all winter.

23

There was no one washing in the stone laundry basin by the town hall on Sunday morning. It was too early for the sun to crackle the water's surface, and anyone who would usually be doing laundry there was either dressing for church, or still in bed.

"The Mass is at 9:30 on Sunday morning," Monsieur le curé had said, standing in his curry-coloured courtyard.

"We would like to come," I replied, "but don't forget that we are only Protestants."

"Of course, of course, I know that. It would be only to come. Only to come."

The Café de la Poste was shuttered tight in the grey morning light, but we could see that the bakery at the end of the street was open. I was thinking ahead. All we had was a fifty-franc note, and we knew there would be a collection. We would have to find change.

"There's no bread today," said Madame Galon. When she heard us opening the front door, she had shuffled out of her silent kitchen to her post by the cash register. "It's Sunday. The oven is cold, so there's no bread. If you want bread, you'll have to take yesterday's."

"We don't want bread. We still have half a loaf from yesterday. We're sorry. But we only need change. Have you any?"

"How much?"

"It's for the Church. For the collection."

"Oui oui oui, how much?"

"Fifty francs."

"Five thousand francs. Five thousand. . . ." Like many of the old French people, she could only visualize money in terms of old francs.

"Yes, I have enough," she said finally. She gave us the money.

"Merci Madame."

"Ça ne'rien. Allez-au'voir."

The little winding streets behind the bakery were too narrow for a car. We followed some village children who told us they knew a short cut to the church. We listened to their footsteps and laughter, confined in the spaces between the buildings. It was damp. Up above us, the bells of the church were sounding a last urgent call to the villagers.

"Hurry, Monsieur! Hurry, Madame! It is almost time!" They ran on ahead up the steep sidewalk, leaving us puffing, and wondering how the old people in the village ever made it to Mass.

There wasn't time to look over the wall beside the front door when we arrived, even though the view was compelling. Monsieur le curé was there, standing on the steps waiting for us. He was dressed impeccably in his black Sunday suit. And he greeted us quietly, simply at the door. Our boisterous friend was transformed. He had changed into his priestly role as easily as slipping into a black Sunday suit.

"Go in and get a good seat," he said kindly. "I have to get up to the front now that you are here, and put on my cassock. There are still a few minutes." He turned and left us.

All down the centre aisle of the church, angled along the worn stone floor, portable gas heaters were burning. Like all the old churches, this one wasn't heated, and the villagers must have decided that gas heaters were better than nothing. Monsieur Barruol, who was there with his family, saw us come in and rushed down from his seat to greet us at the door. "Come with me," he whispered. "We have good seats for you up there. Just behind us. You see? Right beside a heater. It will keep you warm during the service."

We watched the gas heaters flickering and flaring, and the congregation huddled as close to the centre aisle as possible. I noticed another heater up by the altar to keep the priest and the altar boys warm. At the front, there were some candles burning, and someone had brought in some green pine boughs and placed them in convenient niches along the side. The church looked far more cheery than I had remembered it.

The spindly old lady in black whom we had seen the last time tugged at the slender rope that trailed up to the hole in the ceiling. The bell was ringing the very last call. She looked at us sharply with a familiar yellow eye.

Monsieur le curé appeared grandly at the front in a splendid green cassock embroidered in gold. His white hair was smoothed down. His face was a subdued pink. He really looked the part, and everyone became very quiet as he closed the small door by the altar behind him.

The white hair of the organist hung straight from under her simple, brown cloth cap. At a signal from Monsieur, she dutifully began pumping the wooden organ, the pedals clapping noisily for a moment or two before there was enough pressure for them to take hold and let the organ wheeze out the first chord of the opening hymn. She seemed more intent on pumping than playing. With her feet more or less a blur on the pedals, she would hold a particular chord down with her chubby right hand long after the congregation had sung past it.

She played with a real economy of style, sometimes leaving out two chord progressions in a row, and falling a couple of bars behind the beat. Everyone straggled on, singing as well as they could, but if they got lost, or if their enthusiasm for the piece was waning, Monsieur would step out of his priestly role and direct the music with his arms waving, and his rich voice booming out, urging the others to equal his enthusiasm.

"And now," Monsieur said, when the music had stopped, "it is time to read the announcements." He shoved his glasses onto his nose, took a little programme off his simple podium, and moved down the steps to a position right in front of his congregation. There was a respectful silence.

"On Saturday, there will be . . . ." Someone threw open the door at the back of the church and came in. Monsieur stopped reading, and peered over the tops of his glasses as the newcomer dashed red-faced to his pew. "Bon. As I was saying, on Saturday . . . ." He stopped once more and looked up puzzled. "Is it Saturday, Madame Bruniau?" he called out to someone in the congregation. "Or is it Friday?"

Madame in the congregation called back, "Non, mon père. It is Saturday."

"Bon. On Saturday, there will be a meeting. . . ." The door clattered open again. Three boys tumbled in, giggling guiltily, and sat down at the back. "Non non non, my children," he boomed as he pulled off his glasses. "Don't sit back there. Come right up to the front here! Right under my nose."

They got up from where they were sitting and edged, embarrassed, to the front. All of them were dressed in rough outdoor jackets for playing. "These are the three boys who skipped catechism classes last Thursday," announced Monsieur le curé. "They decided it would be more worth their while to sneak off to the movies." He looked sternly down at the three boys. "This will have to be reported. I'm afraid I'll have to tell your parents."

He put his glasses back on. "Bon. Now. Where was I? . . . Oh yes. On Saturday . . . ." He suddenly slapped down his programme and glared towards the back of the church. "Now what? What is that noise at the back?" He snatched off his glasses, and marched angrily right down the aisle and disappeared out the door.

"C'est une comédie," someone whispered behind us.

Outside, we could hear several muffled protests, and a loud admonition or two, then the door crashed open, and Monsieur came back in and strode swiftly up the aisle with his splendid green cassock fluttering.

"There were some men outside selling postcards," he said. "Imagine that." He looked back down the aisle at the door. "Come in! Come in, you two! There is room for you at the back. This sermon won't do you any harm. You can warm up, and sell your postcards later."

Finally, we made it through the announcements. We said a few prayers. We started another hymn. To make sure that Lorna and I knew which hymn was being sung, Monsieur held up a small pink paper like the one in our own pew with the words typed on it. Then he pointed to the hymn number chalked up on the dusty blackboard. He wanted us to help out with the singing.

Marie-Claude, a twelve-year-old girl from the village, then trotted up to the front to read the lesson. Monsieur took his seat at one side of the altar facing the heater, staring sideways across the church, looking very grand and dignified. The little girl, with her best Sunday coat and her freshly scrubbed face, began to read. She had a red ribbon tied in her hair. Monsieur sat motionless in his chair looking straight ahead. But as the reading went along, Marie-Claude became more and more excited, and increasingly nervous about having to speak in public, and she began to read faster and faster, pursing her lips, stumbling over some of the bigger words, her red ribbon bobbing. Finally le curé rose slightly from his chair, and coming right out of character he turned to the girl and called out in a loud stage whisper: "DOUCEMENT! Read slower!"

She stopped abruptly. She reddened and turned around in surprise, but he had already slipped back into his priestly role, and was staring straight ahead again, dignified and motionless. She spluttered once, and then went on and finished the lesson at a more leisurely pace.

For the sermon, Monsieur le curé came back down the steps to the place where he had stood before to give the announcements. He talked slowly and carefully, without any notes, with the gas heaters flaring and hissing, and the candles burning. He gave a learned talk on the validity of being a good Christian, and although people turned around to look at us when he threw in an example or two about devout French-Canadian explorers, le curé himself never once looked in our direction.

When it was time for communion, we watched in fascination as he performed the ancient ritualistic ceremony. It was the dramatic highlight of the service as well as the spiritual one. And we watched the villagers, young and old, rich and poor, modern and old-fashioned, line up for their communion, all as simple as children. We watched the very old ones dressed completely in black, fold open their wrinkled mouths in dignity and innocence.

We thought about our own secret ceremony soon to come, where we would stand together in front of an altar in England, and be married.

And afterwards, at the door, we thanked Monsieur for inviting us. "Did you like the sermon?" he asked. "It was sort of ecumenical on your behalf."

From the wall, we could see the five ranges of the Cévennes mountains on the far side of the Plan de Dieu.

"Mon père," I said. "A service like yours, so personal and kind—it could make a believer out of anyone."

24

"You never can say when a baby will be born exactly," said Doctor Cherasse. "But I can tell you one thing, it would not be very advisable for Madame to travel around the fifteenth of February."

"But we have to go to England," she pleaded.

"For business," I lied. As soon as Lorna's divorce came through, we were ready to make our desperate dash to England. We still wanted to be married. We wanted our baby to be legally ours.

"Forget it," he said, striking out our whole plan in the air with a single flick of his gold pen. "Postpone the trip."

"But we can't, really."

"Of course you can."

Moments later, we stumbled blankly out the door into the cold grey evening, the traffic screaming by on the Boulevard Durand, our gallant plans shattered and shot down.

"The hell with it," I said later over a cup of coffee in a bad café down the street from the doctor's office. "The absolute bloody hell with it." People at the next orange table looked up in surprise in the direction of the flat despairing English sounds. "I give up. I absolutely give up."

"Relax," she said. "Drink your coffee."

"I'm absolutely finished with phoning all over the world, writing letters to Canada that are never answered, being backed up against some bureaucratic wall in the middle of Vancouver, B.C."

"But what can we do?"

"Nothing. The hell with them all. We've worked our butts off to please the people who don't count on another continent. We've spent half our savings trying to sugar-coat a happy event that doesn't need sugar-coating. I think the best thing for us to do is just sit back and relax, and have our baby, and to hell with Canada, and to hell with the law." I took a quick sip of my drink. "We'll be married when the time comes and when there isn't any danger, inconvenience, or expense."

"That's all right with me," she said. "I've always said that it's our baby, and our business. It wasn't my idea to get married in the first place. Let's just go ahead and have him." We left it like that, and we drank our coffee.

That could have been the end of the story, if I hadn't written to the Canadian Consulate in Marseilles a few days later. Since the doctor had advised us to remain in France, wrecking our plans for an English spring wedding, I had written to find out exactly what would happen if we didn't get married. The Consulate assured us that our baby would be born a citizen of France. And that news made us very happy. They also told us that we could take as long as two years to apply for his Canadian citizenship after he was born. And when his Canadian citizenship was accepted, his French citizenship would remain intact. He would have dual nationality, and he could carry two passports. That news made us happier still.

Then came the bad news. First we learned that the baby would have to be registered under Lorna's married name. And because he would not have my name, he could not be listed on my passport as my child. If we wanted to take him out of the country, or go to Canada, we would have to apply for a separate French passport. Because of the legalities involved, and the age of the baby, this would be very difficult to obtain.

They also hinted that although the baby would not be the property of Lorna's former husband, if the Decree Absolute were not granted until after he was born, it could be that he wouldn't be my property either!

And if I eventually wanted him to be a Canadian citizen registered in my name, and under my legal care, they told me I would have to go through the long and tedious procedure of adoption. I telephoned the Consulate in Marseille. Just to be sure they hadn't been mistaken in their technicalities.

"Believe us," they said. "You'll have to adopt him. And if you think you've been bothered by bureaucrats and ensnarled in red tape before, wait until you try to get him adopted!" Their advice for us was to get married before the baby was born. At any cost.

Almost before we could assimilate all that had happened to us, we found ourselves back in the centre of a colossal legal tangle. Anything we could do to extricate ourselves from the mess was still completely dependent on the Decree Absolute coming through promptly on February 12th. By then we would have done our penance. We would have waited the extra three months that the judge in Vancouver had recommended. And in the meantime, all our hopes and fears and ambitions and plans were being tossed up and down every which way, with every new bit of information we received. If we hadn't been determined to live in France, and work there, and have the baby there, we would have surely gone home.

My father was the next to get in touch with us, bearing more bad news. He told us that we had made yet another mistake: apparently in these divorce cases, it isn't enough just to sit out the three months and then get the Decree handed down automatically. "It would probably take at least another month after that," he wrote. Apparently, even if our lawyer applied for the Decree right on February 12th, the officials would still have to make a painstaking search all up and down the courts of British Columbia just to make sure that an appeal had not been launched somewhere by Lorna or her husband. And that sort of search is never hurried.

Fortunately for us, my father took the matter into his own hands. "I have instructed your lawyer to draw up a pair of documents which both Lorna and her husband can sign, stating that they have not, and will not contest the case. By signing these papers now, your lawyer can pare as much as a month off the time you must wait. You'll be receiving your copy of this paper from him in a very few days," he wrote. "And I advise you to sign it and send it back immediately. Lorna's husband has apparently already agreed to sign."

My father seemed to think that we could be married in time. And, like the Consulate, he thought it would be strongly advisable. His letter came to us before Christmas. If the lawyer really worked fast, we could still fly up to England, wait fifteen days to be classed as temporary residents, and still have enough time to be married before flying back to France for the baby's birth. It would be a last ditch attempt, but we were determined to try it. Doctor Cherasse would never be the wiser.

25

"Where on earth did you get that coat?" I asked. I had recognized the nose and tinted glasses of Monsieur Barruol, buried deep in an immensely grey uniform. His woollen helmet was pulled down over his head, leaving an opening for his nose and eyes like a letter slot in the front.

"It's my Mistral coat," he answered proudly. He stood wide and grey in the doorway, so bundled up that his arms refused to hang at his sides. Instead, they seemed to grow out and down from his shoulders like a child's dressed to play in the snow. "I've owned this coat for eighteen years. It's the warmest coat I ever had."

"It must weigh thirty pounds!"

"At least." He pulled off his hat in the hallway. "But on a day like this you need it."

"Is it bad out?"

"Bad? The Mistral blew a five-ton truck over on its side on the Autoroute last night. It's not a good day for driving." He struggled out of his coat and looked around the room. "Where is Madame?" he asked confidentially.

"Out driving," I said. I laid the coat on the couch. "She does the shopping by herself now, while I stay home and work here at my little desk."

"I see. But it's still a bad day. You should warn her when she gets back."

"I will," I said, ignoring his baffling logic. I pulled two chairs up to the dining-room table. "Sit down, Monsieur."

"I can't stay long. I just came over to look at your plans."

"Plans?"

"Oui, Monsieur Brown, for your berceau. The cradle for your baby. You told me you had made some drawings. So, since I used to be a cabinetmaker before I was married, I thought I'd better have a look."

"Ah bon!"

I had never built anything in my life. I didn't have the vaguest idea where to begin, but I did know how to draw plans. And I had decided a few weeks before that I would build a large berceau for Lorna for Christmas. One dark evening, I had hiked down to the Barruols and had taken a long look at one of Monsieur's books on Provençal furniture. Then I trudged home, filled with ideas, and worked out a set of drawings for a cradle in the Provençal tradition.

Secretly, I had hoped that Monsieur Barruol might volunteer to help me. I knew that it would be difficult if not impossible for me to build it by myself. Especially in time for Christmas. And evidently, he was at least interested. Or he wouldn't have walked a third of a mile in a heavy Mistral just to look at the plans.

"Very nice," he said. "Very nice." He turned the page. "I can see where I will make it a little more beautiful there," he said, pointing to the tops of the four corner posts. "And a little simpler there. I know a way that it could be made more easily."

"You mean, you will help me build it?" I could visualize the fine touch of a master craftsman on the cradle.

"Of course," he said simply. "I'm also going to supply the wood. I have some special African wood we will use. Very beautiful."

"But Monsieur, that would be too kind of you. It's too much."

"Non non," he said gently. "In the Provence, it is traditional for one to give a gift to a new baby. My helping you with the berceau is my gift."

"I still say, you are too kind."

"Non, it is not kindness," he said kindly. "It is tradition." He stood up suddenly and reached for his coat. "Anyway, I just came over to see the plans today. Just to see what they are like. Like you, I'm very busy preparing for Christmas." He fastened up the enormous buttons on his coat and tugged the heavy woollen helmet back down over his head. "We will begin tomorrow. You may come by my workshop about nine, and we will commence."

"All right Monsieur, I'll come. And thank you. It will be a great pleasure." I opened the door and he stepped out.

Outside the Mistral was howling. He ducked his head into the wind, and turned back to face me at the door. "And you may stop calling me 'Monsieur' now," he shouted through the helmet and above the wind. "We have been friends now for many months. I would prefer it if you would call me . . . Henri."

Late in the afternoons, when I had finished my work for the day, Lorna and I would drive into town to do our Christmas shopping. It had been cool for several days after the Mistral had come, and there had been a frost a while back. We had seen the harvesters out on ladders in the olive groves laboriously picking the dark olives one by one. We wondered whether Monsieur le curé had picked his.

The olive oil at the Olive Coopératif at Beaumes-de-Venise was labelled, optimistically enough, Extra Vierge, or "Extra Virgin." It was very famous in the area. When we went there to buy oil for ourselves, we had to bring our own bottle. "We sell olive oil. Haute qualité," Monsieur le patron had said. "Not bottles."

We saw the black olives tumble hot and steaming down from the grenier which is above the Cooperative, and into the crushers. They are hot because they have been lying close together for several days under the immense pressure of their own weight, and because they are beginning to ferment. The crushers are mammoth wheels of solid granite, weighing three tons apiece. They rumble around in tight circles on a granite base, smashing everything under them: just as they did when the olive presses were water-powered, and just as they did before that, when they were powered by oxen.

Monsieur le patron showed us how the olives are shovelled up into hemp mats when they have been well broken up—mats much like the ones used in wine presses. They are stacked dozens deep. Then the hydraulic pressure is turned on, and a cloudy yellow juice steams and bubbles out of the pressings and pours into cement troughs in the floor.

This cloudy liquid is half oil and half water. It is separated in a machine like a cream separator that works by centrifugal force. When the oil is taken away from this machine, it is still yellow and frothy, but it has a viscosity exactly the same as the finished product.

We were told that they put the oil into their enormous cuves or vats to let it settle for fifteen days. Then they filter it. What is left is stored in other cuves until it is sold.

We handed le patron our empty litre bottle when we went into the Coopératif before Christmas. We followed him back to the gleaming blue cuves at the rear of the building, where he drew off a litre of the green gold liquid. Then he selected a fresh cork for us that would fit our bottle, hammered it home, and we all held the bottle up to the light to admire the colour and the clarity.

"It's Extra Vierge, eh?" I asked.

"Oui, Monsieur. It is the best," he replied gravely.

Every day for a week, I padded down the narrow yellow path that paralleled the stream in front of our house. I followed it through the woods that were green and tropical even in winter, and passed the place where our water fell sparkling twenty feet into a steep-sided gorge. I pushed open the high wooden gate at the other end of the path, and tramped up to the workshop of Henri Barruol.

Every morning, we worked on the berceau. When it was cold, we sat close to the sawdust-burning stove, where the rusty chimney-pipe creaked up towards the ceiling. When it was warm, we worked outside, sitting on the stones that were by the door, feeling the morning sun.

As often as we could find an excuse, Lorna and I would go into Carpentras in the evenings to buy our small clay santons one by one for our crèche, or to buy other decorations or Christmas foods. The streets were teeming with people in the evenings, and the shop windows crammed with things to buy.

On the narrow side streets, one of them covered over with a glass arch to protect it from the weather, hundreds and hundreds of paper lanterns were strung. They gave off a rich warm light, and were painted all colours.

The grocery stores were filled with chocolates and special cakes. Everyone stocked up on chocolates for the Christmas holidays. The cheese stores had succulent displays. Our favourite butcher shop had splendid little coquelets, which are baby roosters, wrapped in bacon and ready to roast. All of their cut meats and rabbits and ducks were garnished with roses. They had made a paté out of a pheasant by grinding up all the meat on the bird, adding secret spices and sauces of the house, and baking it for a long time in a deep narrow dish. When it was finished, they had reassembled the feathers of the pheasant around the paté and cleverly tied in the wings and the head, until it looked like a live pheasant sitting in the window. They did the same thing with some of the smaller birds. They also made a large round sausage of pork the same diameter as a pig's body, and then put a real pig's head and forefeet at one end, and a real hindquarters at the other, and shaped the whole thing so that it looked like a complete suckling pig, with "Joyeux Noël" written on its back. Outside, all types of game birds and rabbits were hanging on hooks, as well as special sausages of the house.

All the stores that sold santons had immense displays. It was possible to buy them costing anything from 20¢ up to about $20 apiece. The $20 ones were exquisitely hand-carved. Skilled artisans called santoniers labour all year round making santons, and when Christmas comes, all their crafts are on display in nearly every store. Some of the towns, like Séguret, had santon exhibitions. And Marseilles had a six-day Santon Fair, with street after street jammed with hundreds of thousands of them.

In the countryside, on the roads, all the towns were turning on their summer tourist lights for the coming Christmas festival. Vacqueyras, Gigondas, Sablet, Rasteau, Vaison-la-Romaine—all were lit up orange or yellow or pale blue, looking like feudal islands at night.

It had been Gigondas that had first erected huge tourist lights—that had been several years ago. They had decided that they should show off their mediaeval ruins, their Chapelle de St. Cosme, and their church with the marzipan roof. And because Gigondas was a fairly rich town even then, with a wine that was known all over Europe, there probably wasn't too much of a problem about money. So they strung up a massive system of floodlights with great cables running from one light to the next, and an enormous master switch-box.

It is not difficult to imagine the dark looks on the faces of the people in the surrounding villages that first night when the Mayor of Gigondas triumphantly threw the switch. Gigondas was lit up for all the world, and the rest of the villages were lost in darkness. Since there has always been intense rivalry among the villages it wasn't long before the other towns angrily whipped up their local Chambers of Commerce. They raked through their municipalities with public subscriptions so that they too could follow suit, and light up their own villages and scenic attractions.

For weeks before Christmas we watched what now had become annual rivalry. Gigondas would snap on their Chapelle de St. Cosme switch. Sablet would retaliate by lighting up their tower. Finally, every town had every light they could lay their hands on played up onto their ruins, with the rheostats jammed wide open.

The road that wound up from our village to the courtyard behind the church was not lighted. But the belfry and the façade of the church were lit up in orange, and unlike the notoriously garish lights around the rest of our village, the lights on the church were small and delicate and placed in corners—like candles. We could see the two massive bells in the tower corroded green. We stood at the edge of the wall in the hard clear air, and looked out at the other villages on the Plan de Dieu.

"What are you doing in Henri's workshop every day?" she asked.

"Never mind. It's for Christmas. You'll find out soon. Do you know? He's a real craftsman. He has a genuine seventeenth-century lathe in his workshop that he uses every day. As far as he knows, it's the only one in the country, other than the one in the Paris museum."

"Imagine. But what are you making?"

"Never mind. All I'll tell you for now is that we're using that seventeenth-century lathe. You remember that when the time comes."

"I will."

Below us, the streets of Gigondas were illuminated by antique street lights that looked like lanterns. We heard a door slam, and someone cough. A television was playing somewhere, but there were no visible signs of life. The air was dead still. Hard.

"It's so perfect, and the air is so clear, that it looks unreal." I reached around her, over her grey cape and pulled her close under my arm to keep her warm. We both looked down.

"I'll hate to leave," she said suddenly. "Even for the three weeks when we have to go to England to get married."

"The time there will go fast."

"Not for me. I'll hate to leave."

"You know what the village looks like to me right now?" I asked, changing the subject.

". . . No."

"It looks like a model, down there. A perfect, miniature scale model, all lit up and on display."

"You're right," she said softly, catching on immediately. "Something in a darkened store window for children to look at."

A breeze stirred momentarily, clattering the branches below us, shaking silver water droplets to the ground. And then, once again, it was very quiet.

26

In the distance, in the early morning of the day before Christmas, we could hear the distinct heavy rumbling of a truck approaching. I had just poured the coffee. Lorna padded in with a plateful of croissants that she had heated in the oven, and as we sat down, we heard the sounds of the truck slowing, and then gears being ground and wheels being turned as it was manhandled into place beside our mailbox. There were a half-dozen stuttering honks on the horn and the sounds of doors slamming, and much laughter.

"Why, it's the garbage truck," she said, looking out the window. "They're early."

We liked our garbage men. They were fast, friendly, and capable, and they came three times a week. A whole municipality can be judged on the calibre of its garbage men, or so I thought early that morning.

"And there's Monsieur Granier, the police chief," she said. The horn started honking again. "What's the police chief doing here?" I was stuffing myself quickly full of croissants. "Jamie, don't you think you'd better go out and see what they want?"

By the time I had ducked under the arch outside, they were all scrabbling down the laneway to meet me—the two garbage men smiling, one with a grizzled face from having missed several shaves, and the police chief, slick and polished, wearing his gendarme hat. We all shook hands.

"You're early," I said to the head of the garbage detail.

"We know," the chief answered. "There are three of us today. I'm helping out this morning so that these two can get home sooner."

"Forgive us for honking so much," the grizzled one twanged. His name was Monsieur Ferrera. He had one of the heaviest accents in all the south. "But it's still early, and we were afraid that all your garbage might not be out yet. We won't be around Monday because of the holiday."

"I think everything is out," I said. "When will you be coming back then?"

"Tuesday."

"But Tuesday's fine!"

"And . . . and then again Wednesday," he said earnestly. Monsieur Ferrera was wearing a grey woollen helmet—Algerian style.

"Ah bon, Monsieur. Your service is beyond reproach." I turned again to the police chief. "Listen, we are just pouring coffee. Why don't you fellows come in for a cup? And a little Cognac as well."

"Ah non. Merci non. Another time perhaps," he smiled. "But we are all in a hurry to get back to our families today. I'm sure you understand."

"But of course." I had been told that, even more than in Canada, Christmas was a time to be spent here en famille. The family is a very important and sacred unit. On any other morning, the garbage men would have jumped at the chance for a little pre-dinner digestif. Monsieur Ferrera's assistant looked longingly at our house for a moment, and then stared down at the ground. "Bon Noël in that case," I said.

"Et bon appétit!" the three shouted back. Then they crowded together into the small green cab, and slammed the doors, accidently hitting reverse on the first try with a lot of laughing, and finally rumbled off.

It was seven in the evening before our own celebrations really began. We put the few homely presents we had for the Barruol family into the back seat of the car, and drove down to the Domaine de St. Cosme for an evening drink. Monsieur and Madame, who were expecting us, met us at the door dressed in their very best holiday clothes. All five children were dressed in their best, groomed and looking forward with excitement to a long evening of eating. There was nothing the Barruol children liked to do more. The sideboards were crammed with chocolates and cookies and special drinks. There would be other guests that night besides ourselves.

We all sat down in the living-room which looks like a picture straight out of a textbook on Provençal furniture. Every beautiful inlaid piece, every stick of intricately carved furniture was made in the workshop on the Domaine by Henri himself. Even the mantelpieces over the fireplaces.

"Every piece fits together like a puzzle," he told us once proudly. "I never use screws or nails. Not ever."

We sat in the living-room and had our first Christmas Eve drink, and I let the conversation and the excitement settle down a bit before I went out to the car and got our gifts.

Lorna presented Madame with a small silver brooch that came all the way from Canada. I gave Henri a very large, very luxurious bottle of rum. "But I will require your assistance with this," he said. "It is too much for one man alone." And we gave all the family a large wooden swag that we had fashioned from things we had found in the forest. The children, laughing, hung it on the wall.

Then came the moment I had been waiting for, when Henri and I carried in the glossy Provençal berceau from the workshop. It was finished. "My heart!" she said when she saw it, "Ooh my heart. It makes my heart beat faster!" Which is all I ever would have wanted to hear. It looked far larger than I had ever figured it would look when I drew the plans. Especially in the confines of the living-room. But even I had to admit that it looked very beautiful. "Oh Jamie," she said. "Thank you. And you too, Henri. Thank you too."

"Listen," I said happily. "Henri and I have made that cradle so big, that the baby will be able to sleep there until he is eighteen!"

"Ahh! Mais écoutez, Jamie," he replied. "That reminds me: while we were working on the berceau, I had an idea. When your baby has eighteen years, I thought it would be a good idea to send him here to live on a farm and live en famille. He would learn French, he would learn the customs of France that you can only learn en famille." He paused to light a Christmas cigar and let the idea sink in. "The true life in France, the family life you see, goes on behind the closed shutters."

"Also," Madame said, "he could learn about the wine."

"What a very good idea," Lorna said.

"Yes, Claude and I have talked it over, and we have decided that it would be a good idea."

"A splendid idea."

"And a year before he comes, we will arrange for little Louis here," pointing to his youngest, "to visit you in Canada."

"Ah! A formidable idea!" We all had another drink.

"And now it is time for me to bring out our present to the Browns," he said.

"Ah non! It's too much. You've already been too good to us. Please, no more presents."

"Non non non non." He reached down into his cupboard and pulled out two dark bottles of Gigondas with his name on them. They were the new-style bottles that he had just begun to use when we arrived. "1969," he said. "A very good year here. The best that I have."

"You are too kind."

"There is more," he said, holding up his hand. He bent into the cupboard again and lifted out a giant green Magnum bottle, which holds twice as much as an ordinary wine bottle. You don't see Magnums much anymore except for Champagne. I could see that the cork was hammered home by hand, and that the Gigondas label had been licked in place. This was a custom bottle of wine.

"You remember?" he asked, peering into the bottle. "This is the white wine that we tried that night not long after the vendange."

I remembered how we had tasted it in the kitchen. It had been cloudy-white, milky and strong. It had stinging bubbles in it like Danish beer.

"You don't have to like it," Henri had said at the time. "It is not supposed to be good. It's too young. It is only to be amusing."

"I like it," I had said. "It's interesting."

"Those tiny bubbles show you how young it is," he had said. "It's still working. If you put your ear to the barrel, you can hear it hissing. I should have shown you."

"I know what you mean."

"Anyway, it will stop bubbling soon, and the cloudiness will disappear. By Christmas it will be seriously drinkable. You will see."

Now, standing by the Christmas table, I stared into the giant bottle, amazed. It was absolutely clear, and although it was officially a white wine, there was the slightest pink tinge to the liquid inside. Gigondas red was indomitable. Anyone can tell you that a Gigondas white wine simply doesn't exist. This was a special treasure. Especially since we had helped in the vineyards the day the white-wine grapes were picked. A rare drink. Not for sale. One of two bottles in the world.

Lorna looked up at the ornate clock on the mantelpiece. "Jamie, we must go!"

"You're right. Forgive us, Monsieur, Madame, but we must leave. We've arranged to go to Séguret for the special Mass."

"Ah bon! You have tickets. Then you must hurry. It's almost time." We all stood around the centre of the living-room a moment longer, admiring the freshly finished berceau. It was capturing everyone's attention. "To the baby, eh?" he said solemnly raising his glass.

"To the baby."

"Pour le bébé." Even the littlest of the children joined us in the toast.

We knew there would be hundreds of people that night in the sleepy village of Séguret for the midnight Mass. It is famous throughout all the region, and people come a hundred miles or more to be in the church on Christmas Eve.

The service is especially "folklorique", designed to raise money for the very poor local church. It is a re-enactment of the nativity scene, performed by the local villagers. All seventy-two of the traditional santon characters of the ancient Provençal village are portrayed, as well as a great number of angels and other religious figures. The villagers of Séguret practise for months to be able to perform in the Bergié. The baker will perhaps play the part of the town drunk, the local mechanic will be one of the shepherds. Perhaps his daughter will be an angel.

To arrange the seating and sell the tickets, distributing them for hundreds of miles, requires a massive campaign. One of the masterminds of the operation was our friend Monsieur Sias, le facteur of Séguret. Monsieur Sias was the busy operator of "The Most Coquette Post Office in the Vaucluse." Even for him, it all seems worth the trouble on Christmas Eve. He stands at the door in his heavy tweed suit with his bald head shining, proudly watching the crowd assemble outside.

The tiny square at the bottom of the village at the south end was a good place to park to keep away from the rest of the traffic. There would be no places at the top of the hill under the ruins, or by the haute church. We were too late for that. We walked up through the fifteenth-century Huguenot arch and stepped back 500 years. The streets in Séguret are still cobblestone, just as they always were, and some of them are barely wide enough for two people to walk in side by side. We climbed under the arching antique streetlights. We made our way up a darkened street, which tunnels underneath the old walls and buildings, and comes out on an open cobblestone street higher up. The narrow arch on this higher street grew in exaggerated Buffet lines, meeting high over our heads. Everything was lit up a pale orange, and the streets were echoing with the solitary sound of a bell calling us to Mass.

"IT IS ABSOLUTELY OBLIGATORY THAT YOU BE IN YOUR SEATS BY NINE THIRTY!" the message on the backs of our tickets demanded. I read this as we settled, just on time, into our chairs which were, not surprisingly, jammed directly behind an arch. For the next half hour or so, long after the Mass was to have begun, we watched the French straggling unconcernedly in. Everyone was elbowing everyone else, struggling to get out of their coats, their voices rumbling agitatedly through the twelfth-century church.

I heard English being spoken somewhere. I didn't hear any recognizable words at first. Only a flat nasal monotone. Like catching a faint familiar smell in the air and not being able to place it for a moment. I listened harder. "Is this our row?" I heard. "Do you think this is our row?" More crowd noise. "Elaine, you'd better ask them if this is our row." An American. "We might be in the wrong row, Elaine . . . Elaine?" An American accent cutting through the French like a knife, monotone, flat, ultra-slow and amazingly ugly out of its own milieu. The French were bounding in now, enthusiastically sitting wherever they could find a space. Like children. "Elaine, I think there's someone sitting in our seats." The accent was embarrassingly like my own. "Why, that man is in my seat!"

The lights flickered once, then dimmed. Then they went out. The crowd became quiet. The performance began. Because we were behind the arch, we couldn't see anything. Worse still, the voices at the front were lost somewhere in the acoustics, so we couldn't hear either. Our ears would have to adjust.

One of the ushers stamped in through the total darkness carrying the brightest flashlight I have ever seen. He stood in the aisle shouting, oblivious to the production at the front, and the fact that we were all trying to adjust our hearing to the faint, distant mutterings. He blared his light around like an indiscriminate laser beam, blinding everyone in every direction. "GO UP THERE MADAME," he yelled. Then he snapped out the light. Total eye-blinking darkness—like after a flash camera pops in your face. Up front, the first of the actors was tinkling away feebly.

"NON NON MADAME!" On came the laser beam. "ON THE OTHER SIDE. . . . WHAT'S THAT? . . . OUI. THE OTHER SIDE. . . . JUST PUSH YOUR WAY THROUGH." Darkness again. The actors. "VOILA! ! C'EST ÇA! THOSE ARE YOUR SEATS." He switched on the light. "THE AMERICANS ARE IN THE WRONG ROW!" He shut down the searchlight once more. I looked at my watch. Its luminous hands were glowing bright green from the intense exposure. Twenty after ten. The last of the French had arrived.

The plot of the Bergié was fairly simple, and it turned out that our seats were far better than we had at first believed. Each one of the seventy-two villagers would appear from the wings, pass down the narrow aisle directly in front of us but behind the arches, turn at the bottom of the church, and then march up the nave to stand in the crèche in front of the altar. This was the sum total of each character's stage movements. But this short walk could take as long as fifteen minutes, since each actor had to introduce himself to the audience and tell what he was doing out at night, perhaps complain about how harsh and unrewarding his life had been, and finally reveal himself as one of the recognizable living santons. All the dialogue was in difficult gutty Provençal instead of French.

When the santons reached the end of a refrain, a white spotlight would turn on high up, and an angel would appear to sing a reply from one place or another in the galleries of the church. The upper balconies and windows were surrounded by pine boughs to make it look as if the angels were singing from the tops of the trees. All the angels were dressed in white, and they sang the choruses in pure French. As the characters marched by, all alone, or in pairs, or even in a group, they would hold running conversations with the angels.

The shepherd struggled down from the hills and tapped past us in the aisle. He was alone, carrying a wood-framed lantern with mica windows. He wore a broad hat for protection from the sun when it was daylight. In his other hand, he had a long staff and a water gourd hanging on a strap from his thumb.

The wood gatherer stumbled in, bent under a bunch of faggots on his shoulder. They were bound in a leather strap.

Then a gaggle of ladies swept past, wearing the traditional Comtadin costumes, white sun bonnets, shawls, and brightly coloured print dresses. They resembled in my mind the traditional Dutch dress. Each woman carried a stick wound with wool that she used for spinning.

Monsieur the mayor arrived with a round dark hat and a mica lantern.

There was little accompanying music. Each person had to sing his intricate part alone, for better or for worse. The effect was electric—and magical. The rich Provençal language, coarse, clear, like a mixture of Spanish and Italian, sounded like harsh red wine. Oil. Garlic. The land. The sun.

I watched the people around me. All the older spectators, anybody over the age of fifty-five, seemed to understand everything. They laughed at the jokes the town drunk made as he staggered unshaven up the aisle, shaking his fists at the angels. They seemed to have no trouble understanding the Provençal. The very old listened nodding, like people enjoying a rare treat.

The young children, who were admitted free, sat on the floor or on the laps of their parents, watching in silent and uncomprehending fascination. And the adults, the people my age and older, were as uninhibited as children. If something particularly interesting was happening, and it was hard for them to see, they would stand right up in their places in the audience, in total rapture and enthusiasm, forgetting all about anyone behind them who might also want to see. Anybody finding his view blocked by a large adult body seemed to write it off with a shrug as just one of those things, and sit patiently silent until the person standing decided to sit down again.

The prompter was magnificent. Because it was only a humble village play, there were bound to be slips of memory and tumbles out of tune. And because of the layout of the church, and the long promenade each actor had to take, it was impossible for the prompter to sit in one place and be heard. The solution was a roving prompter. He followed each actor about a half-dozen paces behind, all the way from the wings to the crèche. He was an immense man, draped out in an equally immense shepherd's cape with an astonishingly loud check pattern.

I assume that he wore the cape in an effort to remain inconspicuous. If you noticed him at all, you were probably supposed to imagine that he was a stray shepherd or something. But the prompter skulked from arch to arch, following the actors with all the bravado of an arch villain in a silent movie. He leafed loudly through his script and peered suspiciously out from his conspicuous hiding places, whirling his compelling cape in the air.

The blind man tapped his way up the aisle with his long twisted staff. A little boy dressed up as an angel in a white robe and cardboard wings took his hand tenderly and led him along.

A whole procession of villagers went by in Comtadin costumes, playing the flutes and drums that are the only genuine musical accompaniment to Provençal songs.

Just at midnight, the Bergié ended, with all the living santons assembled proudly by the wooden crèche near the altar. We knew that a high Mass was to follow in half an hour. But for Protestants and people with a long way to drive, it was time to go home.

We left the twelfth-century church laughing, joyfully listening to all the bells ringing, shouting into the night with the other people who were there, feeling more Christmas spirit than we could have imagined. It was a clear night, and all the villages below us on the Plan de Dieu, strung out through 300 degrees, were lit up with their best Christmas lights—orange, yellow, ghostly blue. These were the villages that had been the age-old enemies of Séguret, making stealthy night raids and slaughters just 300 years ago on each other. Even today, a rivalry and intense pride exists. But on that night, when we left the church, in the short intervals between the peels of the Séguret bells, we could hear the churches of the other villages ringing back their midnight replies.

We returned to our house to open our presents from Canada, and to have a Christmas day drink of the special white wine that Henri had given us.

But we had decided in advance to postpone the next event of a Provençal Christmas, which is the réveillon, or midnight supper. For pampered North Americans, it was too much of an ordeal to sit down to a meal that was supposed to continue non-stop until six in the morning. We went to bed, knowing that our daytime réveillon was scheduled for the next morning, and marvelling at the French endurance. In most homes, behind the shutters, even the youngest children were just sitting down to the table!

Our Christmas day was sunny and warm—warm enough to crack walnuts on the rocks outside in pyjamas. We started preparing our giant feast early, taking breaks now and then to step out and bask in the sunshine.

When lunchtime came around, we had assembled what could be called a fairly typical French holiday meal. We started with the salty-sweet black olives of Nyons, and a paper-thin slice of jambon cru. This is uncooked ham that is heavily smoked and sliced as thinly as possible for eating. The charming village of Malaucène, tucked into the base of Mont Ventoux, has some of the best and most famous jambon cru in the region. They hang it outside the butcher shops there like logs.

We followed the ham with Tapenade, which is known as "the caviar of Provence." It is a dark black paste made up largely of olives and anchovies that comes in tiny glass jars with golden tin lids. You eat this course with butterfly bread and fresh unsalted butter. Practically the only time you ever find butter on bread at a French table, other than at breakfast, is when there is an hors d'oeuvre derived from pork or olives.

We moved on to a lobster soup that we had prepared from a can. But we bought some giant pink shrimp at the market in Carpentras to ease our consciences, and we hooked the tails of the shrimp onto the edges of the bowls all the way around. By the time we had finished the soup, it was time to change wine. We put away our great Magnum bottle of white, and brought out our Gigondas Grand Cru from the Domaine de St. Cosme.

We had carefully followed Henri's instructions for the wine. We brought it up slowly to room temperature over the period of a day. And early in the morning, I had carefully drawn the cork, so that the wine, which had been sleeping purple and dark since 1969, could wake up in time for the meal.

Then out came the main course: a great brown farm duck, that we had bought from our butcher shop in Carpentras with the special recommendation of le patron. Lorna carried it to the table stuffed with bread, apples, walnuts, prunes and the spices of Provence. She had decorated its back with paper-thin slices of fresh Spanish orange.

We ate the duck with the stuffing and heaps of wild rice

on the plate all at once. Decidedly un-French. The rice was the succulent variety that grows in the Camargue on the Rhône delta. The sauce for the rice and the stuffing was a special Normandy duck sauce I had learned a few years before, made up from the meat juices of the duck, heavy fresh cream and brandy.

Next came the salad—a simple bowl, made up largely of lettuce and green pepper. We used our bottle of green-gold olive oil from the Coopératif in Beaumes-de-Venise. You never need much—it is so powerful. We sprinkled the salad with tarragon-flavoured wine vinegar and a little black pepper.

By that time, the afternoon was nearly over. What was left of the Gigondas was put away for the next day, and a bottle of Beaumes-de-Venise Muscat was brought out. We thought it was astonishing that such a very different wine could be grown so close to Gigondas. But it exists, and is itself very famous. It is a pinky gold colour, and syrupy sweet, and is served very, very cold.

We put the Muscat on the table alongside the pièce de résistance: the traditional thirteen desserts of Provence. Thirteen impossible, sweet, Christmas desserts.

We had asked everyone we knew to tell us which desserts actually made up the thirteen. And everyone seemed to be in agreement that there was one dessert for each of the twelve apostles, and one for the infant Jesus. They also represented each of the twelve months of the past year, and one for the New Year. But as far as telling what exactly the thirteen desserts were, we never were able to get an accurate accounting. Everyone was able to drag out an old Provençal-speaking grandfather from somewhere or other who would tell us absolutely and once and for all what the desserts were. And we would go home happy, only to meet someone else's Provençal grandmother at the door with a different version entirely!

But we were eventually able to formulate a consensus of opinion, and figure out approximately what desserts should be served. We sat at the table in the late afternoon, struggling lamely through a course of figs, dates on the branch, walnuts, nougat, chocolates, raisins, pears, Mandarins, apples, prunes and hazelnuts. One after the other. Next came the kaki, which are a bright orange fruit that look like a bad plastic copy of a peach. They are a type of persimmon, harvested in late December, and hollowed out and filled with rum for Christmas.

And finally, for number thirteen, since there was some confusion about the desserts, was a little concession to our own past (guaranteed to raise questioning eyebrows and hackles all over the south of France)—a Crosse and Blackwell's English Christmas pudding with brandy butter sauce.

27

Every morning in early January, we waited nervously together by the mailbox for the yellow mail truck of Monsieur le facteur. And every morning, as the time for the truck to arrive approached, I could actually feel my stomach twisting in anxiety, and my temper and frustration building.

"Damn! He's late again."

"For heaven's sake, Jamie. He's only two and a half minutes late by your own watch. He can't be right on the button every day."

"Makes no difference. He's late just the same. Probably lost our letter anyway."

Lorna had still to sign the papers declaring that she would not contest her divorce ruling. Day by day, and week by week, we had waited for their arrival by mail, and still they did not come. Everything was now up to the lawyer. According to my father's letter before Christmas, we were to have received the papers within a few days. So when the papers did not arrive and Christmas was over with, we were left helpless and frustrated, trusting our lawyer to come through for us, nervously watching our plan to go to England become less and less of a possibility. My work was going downhill. I was developing trouble sleeping at night. I was losing weight.

"I want the baby to be truly ours," I had said. And by the time January was half gone, signing the papers had become the most important thing in our lives.

Finally, when we couldn't wait any longer, I cashed one of the very last of our traveller's cheques, and walked down to the post office and called Canada once more. Eventually the mystery of the missing documents was solved. It seemed that there was a ground controller's strike in progress in Canada. And apparently, if you can't control the ground, you can't fly a plane. So all Canadian air mail was stopped.

We found out that our lawyer had dropped the papers into the mail anyway, although I figured that considering the urgency of the case, he could have easily had a courier drive the few miles from Vancouver across the border to drop them in a mailbox in the United States. What were a few extra miles, when we were prepared to make a potentially dangerous trip all the way to England?

In any case, our minds were put at ease by the phone call. At least the papers were in the mail. I relaxed a bit, and settled down for a long wait.

It really was long. The papers didn't arrive in our mailbox, innocuously wrapped in a tattered brown envelope, until February the 8th! Four days before the Decree Absolute could have been asked for in any case. They were useless to us. It was too late to go to England.

"There is only one thing left to do," Lorna announced. "We must go down and tell our troubles to the Mayor. At least our baby will be born a French citizen. If we tip the Mayor off in advance, he will have time to help us unravel all the red tape involved in getting him a French passport, after his birth is registered in Gigondas."

"But the whole village will find out that we're not really married. This isn't Yonge Street in Toronto, you know. These are simple country farmers. They'd freak out. What would the Barruols say?"

"I doubt if they'd find out," she said. "Monsieur le maire is our friend. I'm sure he will be very discreet."

Monsieur le maire ran his wine business informally, permanently decked out in turtleneck sweaters and long curling hair, perennially smiling at the little problems of the world, intelligent and gregarious. His wine house was one of the best in the Commune of Gigondas. His wine, Domaine de Longue-Toque, was distributed even in North America.

He had only been in the wine business for ten years. Before that, he had been a professional soldier, fighting in the Second World War, all over Indo-China including Viet Nam, and then all over Africa. He retired as a major to the peaceful life of a professional viticulteur. "I got tired of all those colonial wars," he said, smiling tiredly, "they were so . . . pointless." His lapel showing the tiniest flash of red from his Legion of Honour medal.

He was the only French citizen in the entire area who could speak English with any degree of fluency, and he practised it proudly on us whenever we visited. He was also a great patron of the arts, very sympathetic to all artists and their causes, and he was graced with a keen legal mind. There was no one who could have understood our problem better.

"I am sorry to bother you," I told him in his office. "But a matter of great importance has come up."

"Yes?" he said smiling. The Legion of Honour ribbon flashed at me, and oil paintings stared brightly-coloured from his walls.

". . . I must ask you to keep the information I will divulge strictly confidential." I had looked up the word for "confidential" in my dictionary before we had left for the appointment.

"Of course, of course. Go on."

"The problem is . . . ." I was afraid to say it. No one knew. He would be the first to know. I looked quickly at Lorna for reassurance. "Madame and I . . . that is . . . Lorna and I . . . we are not married." I had said it.

"Yes yes, go on." He didn't budge. I had said it, and he didn't pass out on the floor or fall into a fit. He didn't even raise a majorly eyebrow. "And what is the problem?"

I poured forth the whole story then: how we had lived together for a long time, how we had always considered ourselves married, how the baby was coming very soon, how nothing could be done to keep him from being illegitimate, how . . . .

"But why don't you get married in the Canadian Consulate?" he asked immediately.

"Pardon?"

"Why don't you get married in the Canadian Consulate in Marseilles? You don't have to go all the way to England to get married. Just drive down there. It's only sixty miles. It's officially Canadian soil. You can be married right here."

"We . . . we . . . never thought of it."

"It would be so much simpler."

"But of course!" I laughed. All the lawyers. Three separate law firms. One judge. The French Consulate in Toronto. The Canadian Consulate in Marseilles. No one had thought of such a simple solution. It took Monsieur, the ex-major, full time winemaker, part-time mayor of Gigondas to unravel the whole problem in an instant. "But of course!"

"I'll call the Consulate and find out for sure," he said.

It all seemed so easy. Everyone had seemed so far away and out of touch when we had waited by our mailbox. And here was the Mayor picking up his telephone and calling Marseilles. Just like that. The call went through immediately to Monsieur Lapointe, the Vice-Consul, and head of operations there.

Monsieur Lapointe had heard about the letter we had sent the Consulate in the late fall, so he knew vaguely about our problem. He was very sympathetic. "No," he answered. "We never do any marrying here. We have always sent Canadians down the street to be married at the British Consulate. But do you know, Monsieur le maire? They have been so swamped with people who wanted to be married that they have had to give it up. The Consulate was becoming overrun with hopeful young couples. So now, we have a special dispensation which allows me to give you permission to marry these two Canadians, Monsieur."

The Mayor was thinking fast. "But that leads to another problem right away," he said. "According to French law, we must wait 300 days after a divorce is finalized before we can marry someone."

"No problem. No problem, Monsieur Chapalain. As of January of this year, I can give you a special dispensation which will allow you to marry according to the dictates of the French law, but following the will of the Canadian law! It is simple."

"You are right," he replied. "It is simple."

"You just send me down the copy of the Decree Absolute when it comes, and I will gladly give my permission," Monsieur Lapointe said.

"Thank you, Monsieur le Vice-Consul."

"It is nothing."

The Mayor put down the telephone, and I put down the little extra earphone I had been listening on. "Well," he said. "There you have it. You get the Decree in the mail, and I, Roger Chapalain, will marry you. Right here in Gigondas!" It had been something that at one time didn't matter. But now, to be married, to start our little family off on the right foot, had become the most important thing in our lives. I reached over and touched Lorna's hand. We both had tears in our eyes. To be married in Gigondas meant a great deal to us too. We mumbled some sort of thanks to Monsieur Chapalain.

"It is nothing," he answered, his own eyes flooded with tears.

So that night, we were back in action. We spent what was left of our very last traveller's cheque, and telephoned Vancouver once more. At 7:00 p.m. our time, it was only 11:00 in the morning there.

"Do you still need those papers?" I asked the lawyer when we finally got through. "It's so late. The Decree can be applied for in a few days anyway."

"Yes. They'll still be a help." He sounded crackly and far away.

"How long will it take you to get the Decree signed?"

"I can get it done the same day the papers arrive in my office. Everything else is ready here. And the strike is over. Just sign the papers in front of a public notary, and mail them to me."

"We're really in a hurry," I shouted into the telephone. "Please go as fast as you can."

"Oh don't worry, I will." He crackled cheerfully. He sounded like an ambitious young lawyer on his way up. "You just be sure they're witnessed by a public notary."

In the morning, the rain was falling in great translucent sheets. We had made an appointment by telephone to see the public notary of Vaison-la-Romaine at 10:00 a.m. When we drove down the hill in front of our house, and down through the Andalusian village of Sablet, the water was running in rapids across the road, leaving runnels of sand and gravel on the asphalt for us to traverse, like the worst part of an obstacle course.

We sank down into the deep leather chairs of Monsieur le notaire, with our hair hanging dark and flat and stringy at the sides of our heads. We smelt very wet, and were breathing heavily. In the other room, the typewriters of the three secretaries tapped steadily, reminding me of the insistent sound of teletypes in a newsroom. Outside, the rain was still falling hard, and collecting in pools in the inner court.

Monsieur le notaire sat across from us behind his imposing wooden desk, painstakingly reading his mail, ignoring us completely, looking old and dignified and a little crusty, as if he had never been wet in his life. I remembered, as we waited, having seen the prominent gold seals placed above his gate at the end of his garden, telling anyone who passed by that the public notary lived inside. They were as large as pizza platters. We had half expected an honour guard to strut out of the bushes, pumping out the first few bars of the Marseillaise as we slopped through the mud puddles on the way to the notary's door.

"Now," said the notaire finally. "What do you want?" He looked up over the tops of his glasses at us disagreeably.

"We want you to witness a signature for us, Monsieur le notaire." I said. "And then, if you would be so kind, to place your seal on these documents."

"What documents? What are they about?" He drummed his fingers on the desk, already bored with us.

I went through the whole story yet again about how we were not married, and how we wanted to be, and how our baby would have so much trouble getting a passport if we weren't, and how everything depended on our mailing the papers that very morning. The whole time I told the story, the notary stared disapprovingly down his glasses at Lorna's swollen belly. We both sank deeper into the leather chairs.

"Let me see the papers," he said suddenly.

We fumbled nervously in our shopping basket, trembling, all thumbs, and pulled them out of the plastic envelope we had used to protect them from the rain. As I handed them across the table, I noticed that Lorna's shopping list was wedged under the paper clip, over the first page. I made a desperate attempt to snatch back the list, but he was too quick for me. He had the papers in his hands. For a long time, he stared at the list.

"What's this?" he finally said.

"Oh . . . just a shopping list. Stuck there by accident to keep it out of the rain . . . heh heh." Monsieur who had never been wet in his life studied us, almost contemptuously, for a long time. I could almost visualize the two gold seals above his gate staring out at me over the tops of his glasses. He tossed the list back to us across the desk, and then began to peruse the documents. Slowly. One page at a time.

". . . If you would only witness the signature, Monsieur."

He looked up sharply, wordlessly, and then went on reading. Suddenly he pressed a button summoning his assistant, who arrived moments later, looking horn-rimmed and intelligent, but as nervous as we were. And as if the arrival of the assistant were the exact dramatic moment, Monsieur le notaire threw down the papers and stood up. "I won't sign them," he said. "They're in English."

There was a long stunned silence. ". . . Why not?"

"I can't sign these papers. I can't understand them. I don't know what they're about. You will have to send them back to Vancouver, and have them officially translated into French." The horn-rimmed assistant rapidly agreed.

"But . . . Monsieur," I gasped. "We can't. There isn't time!"

Arching an eyebrow, he looked again across the desk at Lorna's belly. "Evidently."

From that moment, I could feel my temper rising. My back was up against the wall. What had mattered not at all nine months ago now meant everything. For me. For my little wet family. I summoned my courage, I scratched every corner of my brain for every legal term I knew, every complex abstract verb, every bit of good French. I was fighting for my life.

"I will not sign the papers."

"But what does it matter whether you understand what is in the papers? I am only asking you, kind Monsieur, to sign saying that you witnessed Madame's signature."

"And how do I know that is what I would be signing?"

I argued with the able assistant. I debated respectfully with the notaire. My voice quavered with emotion and the weight of the words. And finally, just as suddenly as the argument began, Monsieur le notaire gave in!

"Madame," he said brusquely. "Sign the papers." And she did.

He said a few swift words to his assistant, who disappeared nodding through the double doors carrying our documents. He demanded Lorna's passport, which he studied for a long moment, and then handed back to her. He picked up some other letters in his mail and began to read them, leaving us wordless in the leather chairs. We listened to the insistent tapping of the typewriters in the other room.

After about five minutes, the assistant scurried back, and we could see, even as he carried the papers to the desk, the official red seal of the notaire publique of Vaison-la-Romaine on the bottom of each page.

We found out later that the assistant had typed in a brief

note at the end of the documents, and beside each place that the notaire had to sign. It was written in French, giving the date, and proclaiming that the public notary had witnessed Lorna's signature, but that he didn't have any idea what the papers were about! Monsieur le notaire signed the documents.

That was all we needed. We asked excitedly in the outer office how much we owed. "Nothing," answered the assistant, turning suddenly kind, and shaking hands. "You owe us nothing for such a small act." We both thanked him. We had already thanked the notary. "It is nothing," he said again. "Our congratulations to you both!"

We mailed the papers that very morning in the rain from the Vaison post office. We sent them by air mail, special delivery and registered, sticking every kind of urgent message and stamp known to man on the envelope. And then we settled down for another long wait.

Monsieur le maire smiled kindly when he heard about our difficulties. "But you have done well," he said. "And everything is up to your lawyer now. We must all wait, and hope that the papers will arrive before the baby."

We both nodded. We could tell he was intrigued with the whole problem. "You know?" He smiled again. "It is all like a race, this marriage. A real adventure. . . . You could call it the Grand Prix of the Vaucluse!"

28

Anywhere else, except the desert, it would have been a completely black night. But in Provence, in the spring, even when the moon has completely disappeared, there is still a faint shimmering light from the stars.

"Maybe the Barruols are still eating," I said. I had helped Lorna up the little stone steps by our house while our eyes had adjusted to the dark. When we got up to the road, we could smell the wood smoke from the coals in our fireplace, and we headed west down the road in the direction of the Domaine de St. Cosme. Overhead the sky was filled with stars. The lower, brighter ones could have been ornaments suspended from strings. All of them twinkled and glittered like you always read about, but rarely see.

"No. They'll have finished their dinner. It's 9:30, and the youngest ones will have to be in bed soon." She was wrapped dramatically in her grey Melton cape. We both studied the stars as we walked.

In the inner courtyard of the Domaine behind the great arch, somewhere on the other side of the outdoor basins, a small orange light was burning. It lit up the pale inner courtyard walls in a light that could have been candlelight, if it had flickered. The rest of the Domaine was totally dark.

"They've got all the shutters closed," I whispered.

"Maybe we should have told them we were coming."

"No, don't worry. Like every other family in France, they're probably grouped around the dining-room table with the oilcloth spread, watching la télé."

We knocked on the door in total darkness, and listened a few moments later to the sounds of someone fumbling with the inner latches. The French really bolt themselves in for the night.

When the door opened, we were immediately surrounded with

blinking bright light, and the sounds of Mozart and laughter. Madame and two of the children were standing there smiling.

"But what a surprise!" she said. "Entrez."

"We don't wish to intrude. . . ."

"Non non non non! Entrez. Entrez!"

"We've brought a small surprise for the enfants."

"Entrez! Entrez!" cried the two youngest girls. They led us into the dining-room where Henri Barruol was sitting, both elbows on the oilcloth. I noticed that the T.V. wasn't on. It wasn't even in the room. So much for myths. Henri gave us all a drink.

I reached into my pocket while he was pouring, and found the jar I had been carrying, and slapped it down on the cloth.

"What is that in the jar?" asked Henri.

"Popcorn. That's why we've come down."

"Pompcorn?"

"Popcorn."

He studied the contents of the jar. Some of his children gathered at his elbows to study it too. "It looks like maize to me."

"It is maize. But it's a special maize. You heat it in oil, you see. . . ."

"Oh! Oui oui. I know all about it. You heat it in oil, and then you can eat it."

"That's right."

"You North Americans eat a lot of maize," he said, setting down the jar. "Over here, it's only for animals."

"But this is a different kind! This maize is very special. We found it in the market in Carpentras."

"We told the man in the market that his maize, or popcorn as we call it, was too expensive," Lorna said. "And the man answered: 'But Madame, this popcorn is very special. It comes all the way from Canada!"

"Ah bon." Madame Barruol smiled. "All the way from Canada."

"So we have brought some down for you to try. Especially the children."

"Very well," Madame answered, always polite. "I'll cook it for you if you wish."

"Non non non non. It's for me," I said, "le grand chef, to do the cooking. It requires a special skill."

"Do you have any oil in your kitchen, Madame?" Lorna asked.

"We've brought a little pot of butter, but we didn't bring any oil." She pulled the blue pot of butter out of her cape.

"Of course," Madame said. All French housewives have oil.

"You see, Claude, he must cook the corn in oil. It's very hard right now," said Henri in his most authoritative voice. "After a while, it will soften."

Lorna and I smiled to ourselves. Here was a man who had found Roman ruins in his fields, who was a musician and motorcycle enthusiast, a grower and connoisseur of wine, with a library full of leather-bound classics. And even *he* was in for a surprise.

"Bon," I said, excited. "To the kitchen!"

We settled around the central table by the stove with all the children clustered close. Madame produced the oil we had asked for and some salt. "Now," I said. "One last thing: do you have a large pot?"

"A very large one," Lorna said. "With a lid." We were both enjoying our little joke immensely.

"Mais oui," said Madame. She reached into her cupboard and lifted out a large clay casserole dish.

"Non non, Madame. A metal pot with a lid. That I can put right over a flame."

"Ahhh!" She pulled down a splendid aluminum pot that was hanging on thc wall.

I put enough oil in the bottom, and turned on the gas stove, and poured in the corn. "You see?" I asked. "Does everyone see? Just enough to cover the bottom. You have to do this just right. I want you to see so that you can try it yourselves another day."

"We see. We see," said the youngest girl.

"Now watch," Henri said. "It will soften."

I put it on the heat. And for a long time, nothing happened. We could all hear the oil sizzling and frothing over the flame, but no popping. The Barruol family began to lose interest, and settle down for a long wait.

"Excuse me," Madame said. "Now that it's cooking, and you have everything you need, I must put the littlest one, Louis, to bed." She got up and left, thinking that the most interesting part was over with. And still there wasn't a sound from the pot except for the oil. I was beginning to think our maize wasn't so special.

POP! Five heads spun around towards the pot. POP! Again.

"What was that?"

"Something made a popping noise!"

"Let me look in the pot and see what's wrong," said Henri.

"Non non! There's nothing wrong. It'll be all over the place," I said. POP! POP! Poppity pop! And then it really let go with hundreds of pops going off at once. Five pairs of eyes were very wide, staring at the pot.

"Incroyable!"

"Claude! Claude! Come quickly and hear this!" Henri shouted. "Quick!"

And if they were astonished by the sound it made, they were flabbergasted when I opened the pot and it was full right to the top.

"Oooo!" cried the two little girls in unison.

"But it's incredible," said Henri, who was a man who had seen everything. "So much pompcorn from so little!"

Madame came back just in time to see me pour the hot melted butter over the steaming white bowlful. "Ah bon!" she said smiling. "And what is this? Another Canadian delicacy?"

"Non non, Maman. C'est le pompcorn. It has aggrandized!"

"Yes, Claude. You missed it. I told you to wait. Come Jamie, you must demonstrate it again for my wife."

And I did. I went through the whole ritual again, and all six of them watched transfixed, as if none of them had seen it before. When I had popped a second bowlful, and when it too was salted and buttered, we all sat down to eating it in earnest around the kitchen table.

"I have something for you to try!" Henri said suddenly, leaping up from the table. "Come with me, Jamie."

We went out of the kitchen and down the hall, and through the heavy door straight into the Roman caves behind the house. He led me down a corridor lined with dusty barrels until we came to the end of the row and a smaller barrel right by the wall.

"Since we are experimenting with new things this evening," he said, "we will try my new rosé wine with this pompcorn. Just to be amusing."

"Rosé? You make rosé as well?"

"No, not really," he said. "Just a little bit. Just enough for the maison. This barrel is only for our table."

"I see," I said. I was delighted at the chance of trying another of the special house wines that are not for sale.

He drew a litre of it into an empty bottle. "I'll have to replace this barrel soon," he said, thumping the sides.

"Are they expensive to replace?"

"Yes. But it's not so bad. I don't need to buy new ones too often. After all, this particular one is 110 years old."

In the kitchen we all tasted the wine. It was pale pink, and still.

"It's young yet," he said, tasting. "Still very new."

The two oldest children were allowed to have a glass each of the rosé to drink with the popcorn, and we sat around the kitchen table until it was quite late. Henri told us vivid stories about how his family had fled the court of Louis XVI at Versailles during the Revolution. He acted out the parts of the various nobility and revolutionaries with a wonderful Gallic mixture of accuracy and imagination. He told how his family had then fled to Russia, and had managed to be on the losing side of the Russian Revolution as well, and how they then had to escape back to France, where by that time the heat was off for all Royalists. Like many people in the south, Henri himself was still a firm believer in the monarchy.

When we finally had to go, the whole family came to the door and thanked us for coming and for bringing the popcorn. "It was our pleasure," I said. "It's a fine experience for us to spend an evening en famille."

"That's true," said Lorna. "It's a great experience for us to be invited in behind the closed shutters. I've decided in my time here that the French are not aloof at all."

"Oh, we are really," Henri answered gently. "But you are my tenants and my friends as well. And for that matter, you have credentials that are far better than a letter of introduction from the mayor himself." He pointed at Lorna's rounded belly. "In France, you see, a grossesse opens a lot of doors."

29

"By the authority vested in me by the Commune of Gigondas, and the statutes of the Fifth Republic, I hereby order you both to report to a doctor this very day for blood tests for your impending marriage," said the chief of police, standing in our front yard. "And I further order you to have the results of these tests in the hands of Monsieur the mayor by precisely ten o'clock tomorrow morning. Or . . . ." He shrugged. "If ten is too early, how about noon?"

We had started up our morning vigil yet again by the mailbox. Every day we waited for a copy of the Decree Absolute to come. Every day by ten in the morning my stomach was tied in a series of strangulating knots. In the evenings, the baby was rolling and kicking so vigorously, that we were sure that his arrival would take place any moment. The Decree still didn't come.

The Mayor had planned the entire wedding like an Algerian invasion: ready to plunge into action on a moment's notice. He had instructed me to report every morning to his house after the arrival of the mail to let him know immediately if the Decree had arrived.

Monsieur Granier, the chief of police, pedalled out to our little house in the valley several times, with various orders and instructions from the mayor. And when the Decree didn't arrive on February the 23rd, the day we had all estimated as being the last day possible that the lawyer would need to send it to us, the chief brought up a case of wine on his bicycle straight from the Mayor's cellars. "Compliments of Roger Chapalain. To keep your spirits up."

The days were getting short. "Any time now," Lorna's doctor said. He gave us a special note to hand to the sage femme at the hospital when we arrived for our flying visit.

We waited some more by the mailbox. One day, when the tension was too great, when I was *sure* the Decree had to be in the mail, I walked up to the Gigondas post office and watched them sorting the letters. I watched as they went through about a thousand pieces of mail. Right to the bottom. Our letter wasn't there. "Oh là là," said the Mayor. "Oh là là. We may not win this race after all, Jamie." Even he was beginning to sweat, and he was a military officer, conditioned to tension. In desperation, he sent us another case of wine.

Finally, when we could bear the waiting no longer, I put the grocery money together, and with a silent promise that we wouldn't eat meat for a week, I drove down to the post office in Vacqueyras and telephoned Canada once again. "Oh that," the lawyer said brightly. "Well it took the judge a long time to sign it, you know." We woke the lawyer up in the middle of the night this time. "But don't worry, it'll be in the mail to you first thing this morning. Just as soon as I get downtown."

"Oh là là," said Monsieur le maire, mopping his brow. "Oh là là." He had streamlined the paperwork by this time. And in a bit of brilliant politicking, he had invited Monsieur Lapointe, Vice-Consul for Canada in Marseilles, to a one-man show a painter friend was staging. The Vice-Consul graciously accepted.

After carefully considering all the evidence that the mayor just happened to have with him at the show—our passports, and papers—and considering the urgency of the situation, Monsieur Lapointe gave the mayor permission to marry us in advance! It would no longer be necessary for us to drive to Marseilles when the Decree showed up. Providing the Mayor himself saw the Decree, and was satisfied that everything was all right, he would be allowed to go on with the wedding the very day of its arrival.

And then, on a sunny Monday morning, February 28th, the papers arrived. Unregistered. In an innocuous white envelope. Not special delivery. There were no air-mail stickers on the envelope, but there was a whopping 15¢ postage, and someone, somewhere had fatefully scrawled "air mail" on one corner.

The signature of the "judge" turned out to be not a judge's at all, but only that of a district registrar, and the signature was dated the 18th of February. We had telephoned on the morning of the 23rd. "Oh that," the lawyer had said brightly. "It took the 'judge' a long time to sign it all right. But don't you worry. It will be in the mail first thing this morning." The envelope was postmarked 6:00 p.m. and bore two mistakes in the address.

So I drove down to the pyracantha-covered residence of Monsieur le maire, thanking God for the French postal system all the way, precarious as it externally seems, making an angry mental note never to hire a lawyer again. Not for anything.

"Is 11:30 this morning too early?" beamed Monsieur.

"Non non. Nothing could be too early! Anytime you say."

At 11:25, shaved and showered, both of us wearing the wedding clothes we had laid out weeks before, ready for anything, trying not to look conspicuous in front of the villagers we knew, we drove up to the Town Hall. The Mayor had received a special dispensation from the chief judge of the regional courts, allowing him to dispense with the mandatory reading of the public banns. Everything was to be quite discreet.

Madame Chapalain was outside, lean and slick. So was Serge, their son, our age, a partner in his father's wine business. Monsieur Granier the chief of police was there. So was Monsieur le sécrétaire and his assistant. Monsieur le maire came out onto the front steps to greet us. No turtleneck today. He was wearing his best Sunday suit. "We've had an awful time," he said, his round comic face very serious. "It seems that all the members of the Wine Coopératif had a meeting here last night. And this morning, the floor was covered with cigarette butts." His long hair came down over the tops of his ears, and brushed his collar. "They have just finished with the cleaning now."

The sun was shining and the air was clear. It was the first good weather we had seen for days. I saw a lizard basking on a dazzling white plaster wall across the street. A dark peasant from the village was slapping her laundry industriously on the slippery sides of the open stone basin beside the Town Hall. High up at the top of the village, the bells of le curé's church were sounding 11:30, and three boys sprinted past on their bicycles, with fresh hard loaves of bread strapped to their backs for their mothers. We stepped through the doors.

Monsieur le maire stood at his place behind the great green table, wearing the tri-coloured sash of the Fifth Republic. The sécrétaire was on his right, busy with the last of the arrangements, surrounded by a pile of papers that he would have to read aloud or hand to the mayor. The young assistant to the secretary was sitting on the other side of the mayor. Lorna and I were very happy, feeling special in our very best clothes, enjoying the fuss that was being made over us. But I was so nervous I had to concentrate hard on simply standing across from the mayor without twitching.

"Célébration du Mariage," the mayor began. "Celebration of Marriage. Nous devons laisser la porte ouverte. The door must be left open." Monsieur le maire read the act he had prepared. He read it first in French, as stipulated by French law, and then in English, so that he could be sure Lorna would understand every word. "Veuillez-vous lever. Will you please stand up. . . ." He had worked for hours, long into the night, a few weeks ago translating the act with the aid of an English professor. Then he made a tape recording of an American girl from Orange reading the translation, with an accent nearly the same as ours. ". . . We shall read the articles prescribed by Article seventy-five of the Civil Code on the respective duties of the husband and wife." He had practised for over a week, into the tape recorder, trying to get the accent and pronunciation perfect.

"Article 212. The husband and wife owe each other fidelity, aid and assistance." Behind the Mayor, on the wall, hung the brightly coloured paintings of his friend from Marseilles. There were about a dozen large canvases in the room. I could see that the Mayor too was very nervous.

"Article 213. Together the husband and wife assume the moral and material responsibility for the family. They take care of the children's education, and prepare for their future." I had been afraid during the blood tests. The doctor had jammed the largest imaginable needle into my arm. Everything was happening so fast.

"Article 214. If no contract has been signed between the husband and wife, they will contribute according to the best of their abilities." This was an astonishing clause, still on the books, which went back to mediaeval times when marriages were made primarily for the acquisition of property rather than for love. We had had to swear in the Town Hall that no contract about property had been signed before our marriage.

Why am I so nervous? I can hardly stand up. I concentrate intensely on keeping my fingers from twitching. I always said that when I got married, I wouldn't be nervous. Lorna reaches over and touches my hand. And immediately I feel better.

"Article 215. The husband and wife bind themselves in sharing their lives with each other." We are still holding hands. It is comforting. It is an informal ceremony.

"Monsieur James Eedy Brown, do you consent to take Mrs. Lorna Ingrid Strom, standing here, as your lawful wedded wife? Please answer in French." I answer, too soon, with too little hesitation, afraid that I sound too eager. "Oui." My voice sounds far off, strong, and not my own.

"Madame STROM Lorna Ingrid, consentez-vous à prendre pour époux Monsieur BROWN James Eedy, ici présent? Veuillez répondre en français." Her voice was soft, as if it came from somewhere else, full of memories of all we had had together, confident. Our hands touched. "Oui."

"Au nom de la Loi, nous vous déclarons unis par le mariage." We had tears in our eyes. The Mayor's hands were shaking as he said the words again in English. There were tears in his eyes. Madame Chapalain's eyes were red with tears. The police chief was dabbing his cheeks with a handkerchief. "In the name of the Law, I now pronounce you man and wife!"

Now was the time for the secretary, Monsieur Jordan, to read the complicated Act of Marriage into the record. When he was finished, the Mayor stood up once more and gave a short speech. "The Friends of Gigondas are very proud of you both. We are happy to have a dedicated young artist in our town, and his charming and equally talented new wife, undoubtedly the most beautiful woman in Gigondas. You have told me, Jamie Brown, how your father has always loved France and how he once wished to be married here and to live here himself. I know today you have made him very happy. I would like to say, officially, welcome to Gigondas."

The sunlight was playing silent tunes on the Plaine de Soleil when we stepped outside. Above us the bells were ringing twelve o'clock, and the mayor crept up to me, smiling by the village wall, and said in English in my ear, "Well, Jamie, we have . . . won . . . ze race!"

Monsieur le patron of Le Provençal restaurant knew us well. He had promised to prepare us a special feast on a moment's notice. Just like the secretary in the Town Hall, he had done as much as he could in advance, filling in the blanks only in the afternoon when I telephoned telling him that we were finally coming. After champagne at the Chapalain's that evening, we drove ensemble to the colourful restaurant in Orange.

The evening was cool and clear, like an evening in autumn and we ghosted through the flat white vineyards on the Plan de Dieu. They were all owned by Monsieur Meffre, one of the largest wine producers in the south. We could see the hard stumps of the vines extending in rows to the horizon, the chalk-white soil a pale blue in the evening light. It was like riding across the prairies at night—Toronto to Vancouver on the Super-continental.

Monsieur le patron eagerly brought on all the intricate courses of the meal he had prepared, perhaps wondering as the waiters served them what our celebration was about.

Serge, the son of Monsieur le maire had carried with him a box of Domaine de Longue-Toque, the wine that he and his father produce. And while we drank a unique white wine provided by the restaurant, Monsieur Chapalain personally supervised the drawing of the corks on the three bottles Serge had brought.

The first two bottles, Longue-Toque of '69, we drank with the main course: strong, dry and woody—unmistakably Gigondas Cru Réputé. The last bottle was poured with the cheese course. It was Longue-Toque of '67. "This wine is . . . a little . . . more special," said Monsieur Chapalain in English. "There are only thirty-one bottles left in . . . ze world. And . . . they are *not* for sale." The sommelier expertly tipped the first few drops into a fresh glass for the Mayor.

He swirled it quickly in his hand, watching the colour and clarity as he did so. Then he tilted up the glass, darted down his nose as far as it would go, and inhaled the bouquet. He sniffed just for an instant, without tasting the wine at all, looked sharply up at the sommelier and nodded his assent.

We drank the '67 reverently with the cheeses. There were twenty-two different varieties on the tray. This great wine was fruitier than the first two bottles, but not nearly as heavy as I would have expected.

"The Roquefort cheese is too strong for our wine," Madame Chapalain said sadly. "Don't eat the Roquefort."

Back at the Chapalain's at about one in the morning, our

celebration ended. We drank some Fine Champagne Cognac, and had some more coffee while Serge played back the tape recording he had made for us of the wedding and the dinner afterwards. I had paid for the feast using the money my father-in-law had given us as a present. And I thanked him secretly as we listened again to the clanking dishes on the tape.

The moon shone like mercury on the pavement of the Route des Florets. Lorna and I walked together up the road towards our tiny house. "They really did a lot for us, didn't they?" she said.

"Yes. It was a lot of work for the Mayor to get all the legal details in order."

"No. I don't mean that. I mean, they really made us feel comfortable and like welcome citizens of Gigondas. We've been accepted here, Jamie. And that's the most important part of all."

"I guess it is."

"They went out of their way to make a little private celebration for us. The whole family. They made such a fuss."

I was testing my footing on the pavement, happily feeling the Cognac rolling in my stomach, knowing I'd feel its effects for days, regretting nothing. "For me, it was the best wedding I could possibly imagine," I said.

"And now, we can have our baby."

30

Even from upstairs, where we were busily preparing a room for the baby, we could hear the sound of a small car being wrestled to a stop above our house, then a door being slammed, and heavy feet crunching quickly through the gravel. I tugged open the casement window, and peered out over the three-foot-thick window sill just in time to see the great dark figure of Monsieur le curé duck under the arch into the front yard.

"Bonsoir, mon père!"

Monsieur stopped in his tracks and looked up in surprise at the second-storey window, his beret slouched extravagantly over the side of his head, his cheeks tinged pink in the setting sun.

"Jeemie! You are here! I was afraid you might be out. I have a surprise!"

"Entrez, mon père. I'll be right down." I closed the window, shutting out the cool evening air, and turned to Lorna. "It's Monsieur le curé. Quick! Break out the cookies and Cognac."

"Non non non non, Madame," he boomed in the hallway with his coat on. "I can't sit! I can't sit. There is work to be done this evening, and it will be dark very soon. Quick Jeemie, your coat!"

"What is it? What work is to be done?"

"My children," he laughed. "I have a surprise. It was only today that I remembered it. I was in the library in Carpentras doing my weekly research when I suddenly thought of you, and the baby you'll soon have, Madame Lorna, and it was while worrying about your health that I remembered the source."

"The source?" she asked.

"That's a spring," I said.

"Why, didn't you know? There's a source just a short walk from your house. I had almost forgotten!" He reached happily into his lumpy briefcase and yanked out a sheaf of faded green papers. "And it's not just any ordinary source. The water has great qualities. Look at this analysis made by the chemists in 1938. I just happened to have a copy!"

There were several pages of complicated chemicals and percentages and technicalities, though how valid these would be after thirty-five years, I didn't know. But as far as the French were concerned, Lorna and I both learned that a source on one's property was something like having a private oil well or a secret gold mine. Wine was something you could always drink. But water? Good, clear water with natural chemicals in it was a gift from the gods, pure and simple.

We could remember many trips into the mountains with Monsieur le curé or with Paul Marc, when they would round a bend and suddenly slam on the brakes and stop at the site of a source they knew, gushing from the rocks. Usually we would find a glass or two left beside the water by some thoughtful person for passing travellers to use. We would taste the water, cool and clear, sometimes metallic, while our friends would explain to us the magnificent properties the source was supposed to have.

Each source was apparently good for some specific ailment. One would be good for relieving gout, another for cirrhosis of the liver and head colds. They were really taken very seriously. Our copious French Medical Encyclopedia had full-page maps pinpointing every major spring in the country, telling the reader the best way to get there, and what he could expect from taking the waters. Whether there was really anything to it, or whether it was merely a way of tricking the French citizens into cutting down their phenomenal wine consumption, we never knew for sure.

"Is it a good source, mon père?" she asked.

"Good? Why it cured my mother of sciatica in 1917! It's fantastic! The sulphur content is very high. Oh, it is good water all right. Bon pour le bébé." He patted his stomach. He turned to me. "But come. We must be off. It's nearly dark and we must find this source."

"Find it?"

"I've forgotten the exact spot where it is. There's no time to lose." He wheeled back to Lorna, clutching his beret in his hands. "Madame, if I could have a glass. . . . We'll need a glass to test the water."

"But of course."

Monsieur le curé's Citroën was stacked to the roof behind the seats with digging tools—great muddy shovels, rakes, picks and augers. They all clattered and bounced and hit the roof and the sides of the car as we rocketed up the twisting road above the house. "It is not far. Just a short walk. . . . You will see."

When we were a little way up the road, le curé suddenly veered off into a narrow laneway that we had never really explored. And we started to go down again—down the steepest and bumpiest road imaginable, squeezing the car through the overgrown branches of the trees, easing it over the jagged exposed rocks in our path. Somewhere below us, I could imagine the little source splashing out of a crevice in the chalky white stones, tumbling into a rippled green pool.

"It's not far now," he said. He rolled down the window. "Just a few hundred meters." He stuck his nose out the window and began sniffing. Just as he did this, an incredible, dead, skunky, musty smell wafted into the car.

"Ahh!" the priest whispered, as if the source might dash away like a wild animal if it heard us coming. "We are very close."

He turned the car off the road into an open place, and clattered along over the rocks and roots for a dozen yards until the smell was positively overwhelming. He took one last careful sniff out of the window. "This is it! The source! I told you we would find it easily." And he shut off the ignition and leapt out of the car.

Huddled in a corner by an abandoned building was a great pool of blackened slime. In the middle of it was a tiny lead pipe, hanging just a quarter of an inch above the brackish goo, miserably trickling water out its open end.

"This is it all right." He chuckled wickedly, rolling up his black sleeves. "I knew it would still be here. Quick! Hand me the glass." He leaned carefully over the pool, and then plunged his arm unhesitatingly into the slime so that he could get the glass under the spout.

He stood by the wall with his arms dripping and blackened, admiring the sparkling contents of the glass. He sniffed it. "Ahh the bouquet!" He swirled it and held it to the last of the light, and then he drank. "The body! The character! Truly, this is great water." The stench swirled up around him from the pool. "Taste it! Taste it yourself. It is my gift for you two. It will make Lorna strong for when the baby comes, and it will make the baby strong too. We'll dig and clean up and restore this stream to its original vigour," he said. "It will begin anew."

31

In the daytime, in the spring in Provence, everywhere you look there are sun-browned men in the vineyards, cutting and pruning the vines right down to their twisted stumps. They gather the brown branches that they have cut, and throw them into huge iron burners to get rid of them. Or else they burn them in great piles right in the fields. In any case, the sky all up and down the entire Rhône valley as far as you can see is softened with haze, and the sweet smell of wood smoke.

But in the night, the air can be quite clear. When you pass down the valley on the way to Carpentras, you can only see the dull orange glows in the fields from the fires of the day before. When I drove to Carpentras at midnight, with Lorna beside me wrapped in the Indian blanket, resting on a pillow, a little frightened, knowing that the baby would be born very soon, we both could see the fields outside the windows, dotted with fires, like an occupying Roman legion.

"Don't go too fast," she said. "Don't drive too fast. I'd rather you went slower, so that we didn't hit the bumps so hard."

I went slower, and we drove all the way in without seeing another car. We went through Vacqueyras, where the curé lived, through the main street of Aubignan past the shuttered grocery store that was run by the red-haired Madame Haud and her husband, and then down into the valley to Carpentras. We took the same route we used to take on Friday mornings to get to the market.

"You have a while to wait," said the sage femme in the empty examining room at the Hôpital de la Maternité. The sage femme, or, literally, wise woman, was the head midwife of the hospital. "I'll put you in a little room near the operating room where you can rest. Your baby won't be born until nearly morning."

She led us through the tremendous doors, which were beyond the examining room at the entrance, over to the elevator, and up one floor to the tiny room with the yellow walls. "You'll be comfortable here," she said. "I'll be in from time to time to check up on you. Don't worry."

It had only been late in the afternoon of that same day that Lorna and I had been together, walking along the steep narrow valley in front of our house where our creek spun a web through the trees. We were hunting for wild asparagus, wild leeks and garlic for a spring salad. The ground had been a carpet of violets. The sides of the valley were green by the waterfalls, as in a tropical rain forest.

"Do you think we'll forget the medical terms we've memorized?" she asked from her bed. "It'll be confusing when the time comes, and we'll have to remember them all."

"I'll remember them for you if you forget," I said. "Lie still. Relax. Like the book said." It had only been a few days before that Monsieur le curé had arrived, puffing, red-faced, and in a hurry, carrying the largest, heaviest dictionary I had ever seen. "It's a medical dictionary," he panted. "I found it for you. You'll need to know the terms in French." We studied it carefully, as well as the other book he had found on natural childbirth in France. We studied that, and the book we had bought in England on natural childbirth, and the books we had been given by a doctor in Canada. "Everything depends on your being relaxed," I said. "You know that. Lie still." We were in this together. We had to do exactly what the books had taught us. There was no Canadian doctor to mollycoddle us through. There would be no turning back.

We stayed together all night in the crowded room, with Lorna lying on the yellow bed, and me sitting beside her whenever I could, looking after her just as the books had said. 'Painless Childbirth,' they had said. It wasn't as easy as we had thought.

"You will be in 'the room of pain' before dawn," said the sage femme cheerfully.

"I will be going too," I said. "I'm going to be assisting."

"That is impossible, Monsieur."

"Non non. I have studied all the books. I know exactly what to do. It's my job to comfort Madame and to encourage her."

"It's still impossible."

"I'll be her interpreter if she gets confused."

"It is against the rules."

"Monsieur le Docteur Cherasse, head of the Hôpital de la Maternité, said I could assist."

She raised one imperious eyebrow. "We will see."

When the dawn finally arrived, first with only a hint of pink on the fringes of Mont Ventoux, and a pale grey area in the sky to the east, and then with the first dull orange peep of the sun coming right up over the garrigues, Lorna was still lying in her bed. There was no sign that the baby would arrive soon. She was beginning to have a lot of pain.

"It's such a big baby," the sage femme said. "It may not come until eight o'clock. Bon courage."

Outside, the sky was a true azure blue. It was like so many other days of early spring. The almond trees were past their peak. A week before, they'd been blooming everywhere—growing in straight white lines in the orchards like a Van Gogh painting of Provence, growing wild beside the road, in the forests, on the hills, everywhere. They dotted the countryside and lit up the area in a shimmering bath of white light. "I have to paint so hard, so fast," Van Gogh said of the almonds. "Because they are only here such a short time, and I must capture them."

"It hurts, Jamie. It really hurts. The books are wrong. It hurts."

But the almonds were past their peak. You could see some trees that were still bright with flowers, but they were getting rare, and only lying in pockets. Most of the blossoms had fallen.

"I hope these French midwives know what they're doing," she said. There would be no turning back.

It was the time for the apricots now. They were just beginning. And everywhere we had looked the day before, and even as much as a week before in some places, the valley was turning pink with the colour of the trees. "The cherries will be next," Madame Ughetto told us. "They are the best. My favourites." Her leathery face cracked into a splendid smile.

"Ma pauvre," Doctor Cherasse said when he came. "My poor one." He stroked her forehead. "It's such a big baby. But don't worry, it won't be long. And when it comes, it'll be easy." He turned to the midwife. "Put her in 'the room of pain' in half an hour," he said sharply. I glanced at my watch. It was 10:00 a.m. "Give her a dilating injection, plus oxygen."

"Oui, Monsieur."

"And find Monsieur Brown a lab coat. He will be assisting," he snapped, bird-like.

"Oui, Monsieur. Of course, Docteur."

When it came to following doctor's orders, our sage femme was stringent. Precisely at 10:30, she helped Lorna into the salle de douleur, and she handed me a white lab coat on the way in, without saying a word.

"The worst is over, Madame. The worst is really over."

"But it hurts. It really hurts! All the books said it wouldn't hurt."

"It's such a big baby, Madame. It's very late, and very big. But don't worry. The worst is over." She turned on the oxygen.

"Monsieur, would you please stand over there? That's it. To the left of your wife. You can hold the oxygen mask over her face." She gave Lorna the injection. I was a little frightened.

"And Monsieur, what is the word in English for 'pousser'?"

" 'Pousser' is 'to push,' Madame. Push."

"Ah bon. I remember now. . . . Punch." She cooled Lorna's forehead with a piece of wet cotton. "Now Madame, it won't be long. In a few moments, you can punch."

We waited. She adjusted the oxygen again. She set the stirrups. The sunlight was streaming in the window at the end of the room. "He won't show up until there is lots of sunlight," Henri Barruol had said one day. "He is a true Provençal."

"All right, Madame," she said suddenly. "Now is the time! You are ready. Take a breath. . . . Monsieur, hold her chin on her chest. That's it. Now . . . punch punch punch PUNCH! Encore encore encore encore! . . . Now rest." Lorna put down her head. "The oxygen, Monsieur Brown."

"Oui."

"Now . . . punch punch punch punch PUNCH! Encore encore. . . ." When Monsieur le curé was one and a half months old, his father was killed in one of the first battles of the Great War. He never saw his son. "Punch, Madame. Punch punch punch punch!" Monsieur was left alone in the world with his mother, who is still living, and who still looks after him. "Encore encore encore encore." His mother raised him for the Church. I will tell my baby this, I thought, as soon as he is old enough to understand.

". . . There is a problem, Monsieur," she said looking up. I glanced at my watch. It was 11:00 a.m. "The baby's too big. I must find the doctor."

"Oh Jamie! Oh God. There's a problem. Jamie! Something's wrong."

"Non non non non, Madame! It's nothing. It happens often. I'll just get the doctor. Monsieur," she said to me, "you will be in charge." She pushed out through the double swinging doors.

Only moments later, we heard two sets of footsteps coming: the light footsteps of a woman, and the heavier, brisk, efficient steps of Doctor Cherasse. We both breathed a sigh of relief. Everything would be all right now.

"Ma pauvre," he said. "My poor one. Such a big baby." He smiled and stroked her forehead. He took off his jacket and rolled up his sleeves. He put on his apron, he sterilized his hands, he pulled on his gloves. "Ma pauvre." He turned and gave a whole series of rapid-fire instructions to the sage femme, too fast and too technical for me to follow. She responded instantly, coolly. "Okay, Madame," he said. "This is it. Attack ATTACK! Allez allez allez allez encore encore encore. . . ."

That war. The Great War. The one that really counted. Even now with the prosperity, with the happiness, with the health, the life, the confusion and the almonds blooming, it is still in the air.

"Encore Madame encore. . . ."

When I lived in the north, the church on the corner was full of machine-gun bullet holes. There was still a bombed-out factory like death down the street. There were veterans in slouching berets with both legs missing. There were the signs, all right. And everyone there lost something. And no one will forget.

"Madame is very strong," said the sage femme. "It's a good thing, because it's very hard going."

Doctor Cherasse was not smiling. "Encore Madame, encore!" She pushed again, with her neck muscles standing out squat and red from her shoulders. I will tell my baby what it was like. How brave she was.

Doctor Cherasse stopped. He said something else very fast in French. The sage femme clattered out of the room. I caught the word "téléphone" and then "vite."

Lorna heard it too. "Jamie there's something wrong." Her words slid over me like a hush deadly chill.

"There is nothing wrong, Madame."

"There's something wrong!"

"Madame, we are going to get the anaesthetist. If the baby doesn't come soon, you are going to sleep."

"Oh Jamie. I might lose him. I might lose him, Jamie." She knew what was going on. She had been trained as a registered nurse.

"You won't lose him, Lorna. Be brave, be brave. Please be brave. You trust your doctor. He knows what he's doing."

Someday when the apricots are blooming, when the weather is right, I will tell my baby what it was like fifty years after the war in France. If he lives. If he makes it. I will tell him how brave his mother was, her neck muscles squatting red from her shoulders.

"Madame is very strong," said the doctor.

"Yes," I said. "Before she was pregnant, she did three hours of dance exercises a day."

"I can see that. Otherwise, she would have given up long ago," he said confidentially.

"She will fight, Monsieur le Docteur. I know she will fight."

The sage femme tripped back into the room, and whispered hurriedly to the doctor. He nodded quietly, then turned. "Now listen, Madame. Don't be frightened . . . the anaesthetist is held up. He's in an emergency operation at the main hospital. He will come soon, but you must proceed on your own."

"Oh no!" Lorna knew everything that was happening. "Jamie. I'm going to lose him." The sage femme quickly laid out the cutting tools in readiness. "They can't cut until the anaesthetist comes. I'll lose him!"

"Stop it! Lorna. Shut up. Relax. Dammit. Stop it!"

"Madame," the doctor said softly, "please relax. You must be brave. You must fight now for your baby."

And she did relax then. Her arms slumped. She went limp. She quit talking. She saved all her energy for pushing.

"Encore encore encore encore. . . ."

The double doors swung open. It was the anaesthetist. It was

12:15. Lorna was soaked in sweat. "He's here," I said into her ear. "He's here, Lorna. Lorna the other doctor's here." Another sage femme arrived also, wearing a mask. Lorna didn't say anything or even respond. She lay there summoning her strength. The other doctor quickly rigged up an intravenous unit to feed her glucose.

"All right now," said Doctor Cherasse, sweating. "This is it." The anaesthetist was rapidly putting together a needle on the counter, holding it up to the light to measure it. "Madame, this is it. One more push, and then you sleep." She didn't say anything. Not even flicker an eyelid. "One more push." And she summoned all her strength, gripping the sides of the table so hard, that her hands were bruised for days. "Push push."

"Punch punch punch."

"Encore encore encore. . . ."

"Madame!" said the sage femme in the mask: "It's coming, Madame! You can do it on your own, Madame!"

I looked down. I could see the top of a head in the sunlight! "Lorna! Now! Push Lorna. You've done it. Just once more, Lorna. Please Lorna." And then the baby came right out. Very quickly. And Doctor Cherasse scooped him up grey in his arms and dashed for the side-table. "C'est un garcon!" He pumped the mucous from his throat, worked over him quickly, gave him some oxygen. Lorna was lying still, the other doctor putting her to sleep to relieve the pain. After what seemed like an hour, but was only several seconds, came a cry first feeble, and then strong!

"He's good, Monsieur Brown. He is strong! He's all right!"

The baby cried again. "You can go now, Monsieur Brown. You can wait outside." Lorna was falling asleep, but she saw the baby first. I could see that. "We have to clean up, and finish in here. Your work is done, Monsieur Brown."

"All . . . you cannot . . . everything have," Monsieur le maire had said one morning. He was telling how he had given up his exciting life in the army overseas, for his tranquil but more prosperous life as a grower of the vines. He had said it again when we were afraid it would be impossible for us to get married.

But I stood in the yellow room waiting, in the Hôpital de la Maternité where we had been together all night, Lorna and I. And across the hall in the room of pain, I could hear him crying. Outside the window, right in the courtyard of the hospital, there was an almond tree blooming, white in the morning sun.

I will tell my son how it was that morning. How we were flat broke, with no prospect of money coming in, how the sky was azure blue, how we had been badly frightened. How for a supreme moment we did have everything.